18/5/22

Curious —

about lifeforms (a)
about lifeforms (b) what other
people mean by
lifeforms/
Parental Body?
if possible

Don't Get Your Neck Tattooed

The Z – A of Life Skills That You Don't Get From Sitting Exams

Mark and Jules Kennedy

First published in 2018 in the UK

3P Publishing
C E C, London Road
Corby
NN17 5EU

A catalogue number for this book is available from the British Library

ISBN 978-1-911559-79-5

Cover design and illustrations: Millennial Creative

www.millennialcreative.co.uk

For Thea, Isaac, Hugo and Oscar

Contents:

Introduction to the book	1
Introduction to Milo	5
Z is for ZZZ	12
Y is for Your Life, Not Someone Else's	18
X is for X-Rated	31
W is for Wonga	40
V is for Vegetables	51
U is for U Can Do It	59
T is for Time	70
S is for Smile	79
R is for Response-Ability	88
Q is for Quality	96
P is for Practice	104
O is for Open Your Mind	113
N is for No Time Like The Present	124
M is for Meditation	131
L is for Listen	141
K is for Kiss	150
J is for Job Satisfaction	157
I is for I Am The Greatest	168
H is for Habits	174
G is for Goals	183
F is for Failure	193
E is for Exercise	201
D is for Desire	210
C is for Compound Effect	219
B is for Belief	232
A is for 'Aha' Moments	244
Sometime in the Future	250
Meet the Future Toolbox Coaches	254
Acknowledgments	257
Testimonials	259

Introduction to the book

"The more that you read, the more things you will know. The more that you learn, the more places you'll go." – Dr Seuss (author, political cartoonist, poet, animator)

Welcome to the world of alternative learning and congratulations of getting a copy of this book, ***Don't Get Your Neck Tattooed!***

Firstly, you may be wondering where the strange, yet catchy title came from. Well a few years ago we met a young man who was academically qualified from school and ready to get his first job but kept being unsuccessful at interviews. He was smart, polite and quite well spoken but had a huge tattoo on his neck. He made the decision to get this body art at the age of eighteen and it is probably fair to say that it wasn't his best choice as the tattoo looked pretty awful.

He was sitting in our training room with a group of trainers and students and we were having a great conversation about listening to advice that we wished we had taken in the past. Some of us trainers talked about the things our parents and teachers advised us to do or not to do. When this particular student asked for a good piece of advice in life, the immediate reply from the group was, **"Don't get your neck tattooed!"**

What, I shouldn't get my neck tattooed then?
Well it's up to you really but the idea of the title is to get us all to think before we make choices in life. Some will be easy to change and some could have a long term affect or impact on us. To give a simple analogy on life choices: a neck tattoo would be harder to cover than an upper arm tattoo but removing a tattoo is harder and painful. Some people will think a tattoo looks great and some won't. Imagine losing the opportunity of a lifetime because someone didn't like your tattoos, hey? All life decisions are similar, let's make sure we are well informed of our choices to get ourselves in the best position to achieve our life goals.

You are about to embark on a journey of personal development:
It will be fun, eye opening and sometimes blunt but if you open your mind to the advice and ways of thinking, there are some great tips to be your best self and achieve some amazing things that you perhaps did not think were possible.

This book will teach you things that the education system will not teach you!
Having visited hundreds of schools over the past twenty or so years, I would just like to say how amazing teachers are. The teaching profession is incredible; every single teacher will offer a unique take on life and will impact every single student they meet. It's a unique and rewarding career which involves dedication, passion and a lot of commitment.

The education system taught is, in my opinion, missing a vital subject from the curriculum: life skills. Now this is in no way a dig at teachers because many of them actually teach life skills every day but there are no exams in the education system on these valuable points. In fact, this is to complement the brilliant things that teachers teach.

The education system focusses far too much on final exams and this is not necessarily the only key to your future success.

So, do we ignore what is taught at school?
Absolutely not! In fact, school is the place to learn. It's a place to learn the system and the habits we all need for later life. It's the place to make mistakes, forge friendships, learn how to respect others and learn how to respect ourselves as we grow. Maybe you won't use every single subject in later life but wouldn't it be good to know them in the first place, just in case?

Work on yourself.
If you study any successful people in the world then you will find a common theme, they all read books. We're not talking about romantic novels or crime thrillers, we are talking about personal development. Autobiographies from other successful superstar entrepreneurs, philosophers, celebrities, world leaders, world changers, pioneers and

those who have become successful in whatever they have set out to achieve.

Imagine a teenager is going into their final years of study, they have two choices:

1. Give up on their exams and fight the system.
2. Work as hard as they can and learn habits to help them become successful in later life.

Option 1 is guaranteed failure in the final exam. However, option 2 will give a head start in life regardless of their exam results at the end. This student will have practised success habits that we will talk about later in the book.

Milo, our man.
We live in a world where everything seems to be over-complicated when all we really need to do is follow a straightforward system. This book is designed to make things simple! You will meet Milo very soon but he is a teenager who follows a plan called the **Future Toolbox**.

The Future Toolbox.
It doesn't matter if you're a teenager in school reading this or an adult who left formal education years ago, the **Future Toolbox** is for everyone to build their successes on. Throughout our lives, we have many new and unique experiences that we can add to as we build and develop. It's never too late to start learning new things and developing yourself.

So what is the Future Toolbox?
The car mechanic, the hairdresser, the carpenter, the beautician, the plumber, the electrician, the builder. These people start their early careers as apprentices and learn new skills whilst using a basic toolbox, perhaps loaned to them by a senior worker. As their career develops, they perhaps get their own toolbox and put more and more tools as they develop new skills and their apprenticeship advances. Eventually they become a competent and experienced tradesperson with a great toolkit that they can use when going to their own jobs.

Our lives are similar!
Apprentices start their learning on day one.

3

We all start as apprentices in everything.

Apprentices learn new skills and borrow tools.

Every skill we learn is a tool and our mind is a toolbox. We learn new skills (borrow tools) and put them in to our toolboxes (our minds).

Apprentices become trade people and use their skills and tools when required.

We do not need to use every skill (tool) for every task in life but as we have a mind of information, skill and knowledge, we can use them to make informed decisions to affect our success.

Time to add to your Future Toolbox.

The **Future Toolbox** is a shiny gift to you and this book will give you some tools of wisdom to help you on the road to success.

Please do not think for one minute that the authors of this book have invented all of the great success tips, they have just been passed from generation to generation of successful people, some famous, some pioneers and some just regular people in the community.

Please use the wisdom in this book but learn from influential people in your life. Take advice from teachers, trainers, mentors, friends, family and other successful people that you know. Study achievers and copy their habits. Have fun creating your own success.

"If you want to learn to fly, then don't hang around with the chickens."

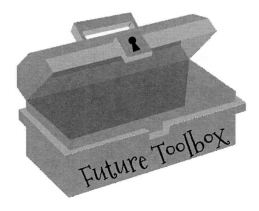

Introduction to Milo

Hello there, my name is Milo and I would like to share my story with you! I'm a regular teenager who does teen stuff. Stuff such as going to school, hanging out with my mates, watching a bit of television and sometimes sleeping, going on social media and a bit of sport – you know, things that teens do really!

Being honest, school is… erm… OK. I wouldn't class myself as "anything special" in terms of ability. I do alright at some subjects and not so well at others. I do like to try hard at times but sometimes get distracted and feel self-conscious about making mistakes. I'm not really a troublemaker nor am I one of those super-confident popular types who is always the centre of attention. In fact, I'm a little shy but am always polite to teachers and friends as well as other adults outside of school. My teachers sometimes tell me off for daydreaming or chatting too much in class but it's never anything serious. I do love being active though and joined the school cross-country team last year even though I'm not the best at sport but do it because I enjoy it.

At home, I live with my mum and stepdad, who both work hard. We get on really great most of the time and they are strict but fair and also quite laid back. My mum is always super helpful to everyone but also worries far too much about me, making sure everything in life is good and everyone is happy. Dad thinks he is the funniest man on the planet by telling really rubbish jokes all the time. Sometimes they are quite funny but most of the time they are terrible. I can't forget my younger stepsister Thea. She is a couple of years younger than me and is quite popular with a big circle of friends. She does drama and wants to be a top actress one day. We get on OK but like most siblings, we argue and annoy each other at times too.

Rico is my best mate and we are sometimes referred to as partners in crime (not that we ever do illegal things) or the terrible twins (even though we aren't related). He sees himself as a comedian and regularly gets into trouble for mucking about and being silly at the wrong times. Everyone says he's a bad influence on me and affects my studies but they all know that he is harmless. In fact, I always love the way he seems carefree and nothing seems to really bother him and wish I could be like that at times. Don't tell him I told you that though, will you? It will go to his head.

Do you sometimes wonder why you're doing stuff every day? You know, wonder what the point is and where life will take you? Well that was the same for me too. Adults always seem to be talking about how much pressure there is in life to be something, achieve something or have something. Now I get called a young adult and have had to start making decisions and thinking about responsibility for my future, it sometimes seems a little scary.

One day though, something changed in my mind and some things started to make sense. It was a Friday and our school arranged a day off timetable. It was heaven, a Friday and we didn't have the normal lessons. We could choose from lots of activities and events were planned to help us think about life beyond school and future options. It was quite exciting, not only because no lessons, which meant no study of course, but the fact that it would be fun and inspiring. I was looking forward to seeing what options there are for me after studying, I mean school is OK but after spending so many years there, it would be great to have a new challenge.

The last event of the day was with a motivational training company who talked about something called the **Future Toolbox**. They gave a strong and clear message about developing your life skills, goal-setting and taking your future into your own hands. With about 200 students in the theatre, it was delivered with lots of energy and we had to do some goal-setting exercises. I'd heard of goal setting but this was the first time I'd really done anything like this myself and it was quite exciting.

There was a man and a lady delivering the session. The guy seemed pretty cool; he was smartly dressed with long hair swept behind his ears and the lady was really smiley and helped us with the exercises we did. Their approach was laid back and fun, he made light-hearted jokes but said some really serious things about life and everything seemed to make sense. I was hooked and wanted to do more of this.

I sat with Rico and another girl called Fidelma, a quiet student who is really good at studying. We really enjoyed the day and had all taken part in the fun and engaging exercises during the session and were buzzing.

"Those who set goals, make a plan and focus on them every day will be those who will achieve their dreams," said the speaker. **"If it is to be, then it is up to me!"** These statements reached out to Fidelma and I, who realised that the things we dream of could now actually be possible. Rico seemed to enjoy it too and made his usual jokes and wise comments when he could.

At the end of the session, the speaker offered for students to take away a leaflet from the table at the back of the room and follow his programme called the "**Future Toolbox**" on social media and the website listed and he said he would share lots of tips and words of wisdom. Why not? We were really motivated and a lot of the stuff seemed to make sense. My mum is always telling me to volunteer for stuff and learn as much as I can about everything, so I picked up a leaflet.

As I read the print, one of our teachers, Louise Lombardi, (or Mrs Lombardi as she's known to students), said, "So ladies and gents, I noticed you enjoyed that. Are you going take this expert up on his offer?" as she held a leaflet to Rico and Fidelma, waving it between them to entice them to take it. Rico wanted to but acted far too cool and carefree to say yes, Fidelma smiled, took it and thanked her.

Mrs Lombardi continued to chat about the session with us and we swapped a few exchanges about what we really enjoyed from the speaker and the tips they had learnt.

She then said, "I would like to chat to you about something exciting. Come this way and I will explain." She led us towards the motivational speaker who was still at the front of the room, chatting to a couple of students. As they wandered away, Mrs Lombardi said to the speaker, "This is Milo, Rico and Fidelma, perhaps they will take you up on your **Future Toolbox** coaching offer."

"The what box now, Miss?" Rico asked, trying to be funny again. Fidelma and I were curious but felt nervous. Mrs Lombardi turned her hand towards us and said, "These are two of our really friendly and hardworking students who could benefit from your expertise."

Rico had started a conversation with someone else at this point so it was down to us. Hardworking, me? I gulped and felt a lump in my throat. It's OK sitting in the crowd of people and joining in but now this was a little outside my comfort zone. The speaker smiled and held out his hand.

"Hey Milo, pleased to meet you, my man," was the friendly greeting. "I hope you enjoyed the session and I noticed you and your mates joining in and giving some great answers."

Fidelma was sort of hiding behind me but he then offered her a handshake too and she was also smiling nervously. He then smiled back, glanced at our teacher and said, "These two could go a long way, you know. Thank you for selecting and introducing me to these superstars, Miss. They have a great, friendly attitude and seem pretty open minded."

He then turned back to Fidelma and I and said, "Here is a gift from me to you if you want it. Take one of those little boxes each off the table over there – inside is a copy of my book, a blank journal and a pen. You will need to commit to following the **Future Toolbox** which will take you on a journey of personal development. You will learn lots about yourselves, build your confidence and self-belief and change your mindsets but before you start, you must make one promise to yourself. I am going to ask you to make that promise to yourself in front of your teacher, Mrs Lombardi, right here and right now, OK?"

"Erm, OK, I guess!" I replied, feeling nervously excited. Fidelma also agreed, after all, we sensed that this was a special opportunity that we had been chosen for.

"OK, it is simple, here goes… You must read a little of the book each day, at least one chapter, and be open minded to the knowledge and advice in there. At the end of each chapter, write down at least one thing in your journal that you have learnt from it. It can be one small nugget of information or a whole page or two. You can write as much or as little as you want. Can you do that?"

"Yes," I replied with a little more confidence in my voice. "Yes I can! And I will!"

"That's the spirit, Milo," said Mrs Lombardi with a proud smile. "I know you will be fantastic if you follow this man's inspiration. I am also going to read the book and fill in my journal too. Perhaps we can catch up between lessons and you can tell me what you have learnt and I can tell you what I have learnt too? There will be a reward in it for you for completing the programme but you won't find out what it is until the end."

I had now made a commitment to a teacher, Fidelma, who was also in, and to the motivational speaker but most of all, I had made the commitment to myself. Knowing that, an overwhelming sense of pride filled my body as I opened the box and peered in. There was a book, a journal and a pen as promised and a few leaflets with pictures and websites on them. There was no backing out but we felt honoured to be chosen and felt ready to learn the life-skills in the book.

"Thank you," I said to the speaker and to my teacher. "I am excited, I really am."

"Milo, good luck, my man," the speaker replied, shaking my hand again. His face wore a big wide grin. "Remember – work hard on yourself, this is your life. No matter what anyone else thinks of you and your new self-development, keep on believing in yourself. Sometimes it will be tough to stick with it and sometimes you will fall back to your old habits but that is natural. Sometimes life will get in the way and things will seem difficult but just go back to your belief. You have no limits to your potential!"

Fidelma and I said goodbye to the speaker and thanked Mrs Lombardi once again before making our way off to get lunch and tell our close friends about the chat and the speaker's offer. We knew some of them would be really interested and some a little jealous because they would like to have been asked too. We also knew that one or two would make fun but we didn't really care as we walked a couple of inches taller.

The weekend was good, a few of us hung out on Friday at a little local food place called Father Russmuss's Food Box. It wasn't like your usual cafe, it had great big sofas, bookshelves loaded with books and it played great music. The owner, Russell, was always good fun and served up good food and snacks. Saturday began with a bit of lie in followed by another trip into town to buy a new shirt before going to a party on Saturday evening. Sunday, another lie in followed by family time and then homework. Booooo!

That evening after doing homework, eating tea and a quick session on the games console, I picked up the box and emptied the contents out onto the bed. The book had a great cover and the title read ***Don't Get Your Neck Tattooed: The Z – A of Life Skills That You Don't Get From Sitting Exams.*** Fantastic, no exams… I'd had enough of hearing about those. Z to A? Well life doesn't always go in order.

I'd made the decision to begin the **Future Toolbox** programme, which is designed to share life skills and I was about to learn the new phrase, "personal development". With the **Z to A journey** on personal development and the help of my **Future Toolbox** mentors, my new life journey was about to begin.

If I, the quiet kid with little confidence can do this, then anyone can. Whatever your age, background or situation, your destiny is in your own hands. **My name is Milo and here's my story**:

Z is for ZZZ – Getting Proper Sleep

"I'm so good at sleeping, I can do it with my eyes closed." – Anon

Milo read the introduction in the book and turned to Chapter One and to his surprise, found it was about one of his favourite subjects – sleep. "Yesss," he called out punching the air.

Like most teenagers, Milo sometimes finds getting up in the morning for school a bit of a struggle. Adults find the same too! He sat on his bed and began reading.

Let us kick off with sleep! No, we are not actually going to sleep now, we are just going to talk about it!

Some teens would add sleep to their hobby list if they could. Are you that person? No problem if your answer is yes – a good lie-in or afternoon nap can be delightful but let us have a look at a couple of facts about sleep.

1. We need it to function. Your mind has to process lots of information every day and your brain does this whilst you are sleeping.
2. Your **body clock** needs setting up like a finely tuned, expensive Rolex watch.
3. According to health experts, teenagers need between eight and ten hours sleep per night (and adults need between seven and nine hours).

So let us **synchronise our body clock** for full effect every day.

Let us assume that Milo needs eight hours of sleep per night, to process all the things he has experienced that day: getting up, getting things ready for school, lessons, chats with friends, decisions on what to have in the dinner queue, facts about homework and suchlike.

He will also have picked up unimportant and uneventful things perhaps, like: a chat with a neighbour, seeing a smart car he likes drive past, someone bumping into him in the corridor, a teacher telling someone off in the schoolyard, a piece of litter getting stuck on his shoe as he is walking home… The brain will store all these useless and insignificant bits of information too.

Most importantly, the brain needs rest to process all the useful and essential information learnt that day. You have a virtual filing cabinet inside you which needs all the essential facts, figures and learnings sorting and popping into little folders so the memory can recall them later. Lack of sleep will throw lots of the files onto the floor in a disorganised manner.

When Milo goes to sleep at night, a part of his brain will act like a computerised filing system and start putting important things where they belong for later and throwing away the rubbish.

Milo started to look at his sleep planner. "It is simple," he thought to himself. "I need to get up for school at 7 a.m. Eight hours before that is 11 p.m." Please note, this means actually going to sleep at 11 p.m., not just being in bed at that time.

Milo then realised that he isn't actually going to sleep until well after midnight, sometimes around 1 a.m. That television box set just calls for another episode or the smartphone screen flashes up another social media conversation that he simply has to be engaged in.

This is called **sleep debt** and it works similar to money debt!

Q. If you borrow £10 from a friend, how much do you owe your mate?
A. Simple, a tenner!
Q. How can you pay your friend back?
A. Simple – either give them a crisp ten-pound note or pay them one pound per week for ten weeks.

"Aha," thought Milo, "I can clear my sleep debt at the weekends. Getting up at midday will solve all of that. Also, that reminds me, Rico owes me five pounds because I paid for his food on Friday at Father Russmuss's."

Money debt can be paid off with cash but sleep debt can't be settled in the same way. For example, if Rico gives Milo five pounds, the debt is clear and everything is back in balance. Sleep debt, however, is not that easy and Milo is starting to understand now why some days feel quite hard to get up out of bed for school. Not only is sleep debt kicking in (going to bed after midnight means I owe my body two hours' sleep if I go to sleep at 1 a.m.) but also my body clock is out of sync.

A Saturday lie-in means the body clock is expecting... a Sunday lie-in. Woohoo, no problem! Sadly, a Sunday lie-in means the body clock is expecting a Monday lie-in and... uh-oh... it is a 7 a.m. start for school again so out of bed it is, feeling tired.

Milo scratched his head and read the facts again, looking for a way to cheat the system, but there didn't seem to be any option other

than to follow it. And there is more; the subtle blue light from a television or smartphone screen stimulates melatonin, a hormone that regulates the sleep and awake cycles. Other factors such as drinking fizzy drinks or eating just before bedtime also come into play.

Sleep Hygiene.

No, sleep hygiene is nothing to do with personal hygiene. It is about having a regular sleep pattern to regulate your body clock. We can improve our sleep quality by winding down before we go to sleep at night. Here are some great tips:

- Establish your regular routine by going to bed at the same time each day and getting up at the same time.
- Use your bed for sleeping in. Lying in bed playing on a device or watching television will disrupt your relaxation, as mentioned above, stimulating the melatonin hormone.
- Develop a sleep ritual before going to bed to help you wind down and relax. Perhaps listen to some soothing music.
- Get regular exercise and exposure to the outdoors (but not vigorous exercise within two hours of going to bed).
- Avoid eating heavy meals and reduce your intake of caffeine, sugar, fizzy drinks, chocolate and all those naughty treats in the hours before bedtime.
- Create a calm bedroom that is cool, dark and quiet. A tidy and uncluttered sanctuary will help too.

Milo looked at the clock next to his bed – it was 9:28 p.m. He would normally have a snack before bed and even have a fizzy drink as a treat. Perhaps it is time now to think about a new habit. He wandered downstairs and chatted to his parents who were relaxing on the sofa. His mum was reading a book and Dad was watching the TV but the book went down and the television was muted. He told them about the day he'd had and the Future Toolbox and they were both proud of him, especially his mum.

"Ah that's my boy," she said raising her voice into an excited sort of squeal as she finished the sentence.

By telling them this, he now felt a sudden sense of responsibility to stick to the programme, as he had done with Mrs Lombardi that day. He then had a sudden realisation, not only had he committed to his teachers and school mate, now his mum knows, he is not going to be able to escape following this through. She will be asking for updates every five minutes, he thought to himself.

After the conversation, he walked into the kitchen and filled a glass with water from the tap before opening the food cupboard. A bar of chocolate sat there on the shelf below the breakfast cereal and both were mightily tempting. Next to the kitchen cupboard was a fruit bowl with apples, bananas, grapes and pears in it. He closed the cupboard after a longing look at the chocolate and pulled a handful of grapes off the stem before heading back towards his bedroom.

"A well-spent day brings happy sleep." – Leonardo da Vinci (Renaissance polymath)

It is now time to ditch the phone and television before 11 p.m. to try to break the habit. Perhaps reading a book before lights out is a better option. He decided to give his first Future Toolbox **tip a go.** It was going to be tough because of the weekend lie-ins but everyone has to start somewhere.

Milo's Toolbox:
Make sure I get regular sleep in order to be able to function properly and I will need to change my habit gradually. Sleep well everyone and dream your amazing dreams. We can bring these to life later in this book.

Milo Challenges You:
It is time to look at your sleep patterns so answer these questions:
1. How many hours sleep do you get each night?
2. How often to break your body clock?
3. What do you consume one hour before going to sleep? (food/drink/media/information).

Log this for twenty-one days and track your sleeping habits. Make sure you stick to this, no cheating now.

Fun Facts – How about this for a sleep record?
Whilst we recommend your eight to ten hours a day, a fella called Randy Gardner holds the scientifically documented record for the longest time a human has intentionally gone without sleep, without using any stimulants. In 1964, Gardner, who was a seventeen-year-old high school student in San Diego, California, managed to stay awake for 264.4 hours (11 days 25 minutes). Now that's just silly!

On the other hand, the wood frog (lithobates sylvaticus), found in the south-eastern United States, Alaska and Arctic Canada is believed to hibernate for up to six months at a time. Now that's some lie in.

When we visit schools, a top-of-the-list dream job for teens is getting paid to sleep. Most people would say, "Don't be silly, you can't get paid to sleep!" Well you actually can. In 2006, hotel company Travelodge employed a Director of Sleep, who was paid to nap in the company's 25,000 beds. Perhaps you could be a luxury bed tester and be paid to sleep in designer beds every day for a month. These jobs have hundreds and hundreds of applicants, though we reckon they would get a little boring after a while.

Y is for Your Life, Not Someone Else's

"Your time is limited, so don't waste it living someone else's life. Don't be trapped by living with the results of other people's thinking. Don't let the noise of others' opinions drown out your own inner voice. And most importantly, have the courage to follow your heart and intuition." – Steve Jobs (entrepreneur)

Milo's alarm sounded and he woke, rubbing his eyes and wondering whether he should hit snooze or not. After a few bleary-eyed seconds, he made the right choice and turned off the alarm, as he could hear the sounds of breakfast downstairs. The body-clock wasn't quite in full flow yet, but it was only day two of his Future Toolbox and he hadn't yet begun to think about sleep debt and the lessons from yesterday – there were more pressing things in his head, such as where he put his school books and his PE kit needing to be taken to school.

As he sat down to eat his breakfast, Milo picked up his book to check out the next lesson, which is titled "Your Life, Not Someone Else's". It began…

This life belongs to you and not someone else! It has your name on it so make sure you are the one who owns it. Insert your name in the sentence below and say it out loud:

"My name is .... and this is my life!"

Milo was not alone but he read it out loud anyway. His younger sister, Thea, glanced at him for a moment, shrugged her shoulders and went back to her breakfast. He wrote in his journal and read on:

You can't be someone else but you can learn from, and be inspired by, role models.

For example, if you say, "I want to be Albert Einstein," then you can't be. Albert Einstein was Albert Einstein.

Now if you said, "I want to be **like** Albert Einstein," that is different and we can learn from people that we hold as role models in our life.

We have to remember that famous people are real people who appear to have ideal lives but we have to realise a few things first:

"Whoever controls the media, controls the mind." – Jim Morrison (singer-songwriter, best remembered as the lead vocalist of the Doors)

19

The world seems obsessed with fame and fortune. Media and popular culture paint a very inaccurate picture of real life; This can be dangerous!

Danger – here comes the truth!
Newspapers and news channels – bad news sells. The goal of the news is to catch your attention and sadly, humans are attracted to drama. Most news stories contain the words disaster, shame, accused, crime, death, murder and suchlike. Rarely do the news headlines report a lovely story right at the beginning and thousands of wonderful things happening every day.

We probably already know that **television** and **films** are not real, they are designed to entertain us, shock us or try and influence our opinions. Even reality TV shows are not *really* that real, they are scripted, edited and then screened with the parts designed to shock you the most. Some scenes are inspirational and some are edited to show the arguments and backstabbing between people.

Music videos are made to sell music. They are edited to make the world look ideal or randomly grab your attention. Some fit the music and some do not. Some are sexy, some are violent, some are meaningful and some are just plain weird. They ultimately cost a lot to produce.

Magazines containing glossy pictures are nearly always airbrushed and do not show the person/place as it really is. They are designed to glamorise and make their subject perfect. Stories are normally bad or sensationalised and are designed to shock and sell.

Milo looked up from the book and thought about the poster on his bedroom wall of his idol – a guitarist in a band who stands on stage, entertaining crowds. Milo loves the music and has downloaded and listened to the songs over and over again. He really wants to go and see this band and has pleaded with his parents to get tickets. Is it wrong for them to make money from their fans, he wondered?

He feels a bit mad at the book at first but reads on as his breakfast continues to satisfy his morning hunger.

The above statements are not saying that all television, news reporters, actors, musicians, sports stars and marketing companies are evil. In fact, they are far from it. If they are passionate about something and they can make money to live from it, then that is fine. For example, music can influence your mood, attention span and feelings, this is a good thing.

Brilliant, Milo thought to himself, he loved to listen to his favourite band and it makes him feel alive, motivated and most of all, it makes him smile. He has watched his favourite film more times than he can remember and it evokes emotions and makes him laugh plus it inspires him to be more like the good-guy character in the movie.

We just have to decide what is important to **our** world, not **the** world.

Our world and **the** world.
Remember, our name is on the life that we own. This is the world that we control. We will call this *our world*. The entertainment world is there to entertain us and there is no problem with this. We just have to make the choice of how much we believe or pay attention to it.

If you watch a shocking programme full of people arguing or fighting, ask yourself, do I want to argue, fight or be a peaceful person? Is this real or entertainment and is it shocking me or entertaining me? Is it wasting my time or is it educating me?

You can ask this of any of the above subjects and when you have answered truthfully, you will be able to make your choice if you think about it hard enough. If your answers are mostly negative, then consider that it is possibly wasting your time or at the very least, be aware that it is not real if you decide to continue to watch.

Milo went back to his guitar hero. Is the music shocking, he asked himself! Well, it isn't really, it has good lyrics and tunes and I like it. Is it real life or entertainment? Easy – it is entertainment, although some of the words of the songs are quite inspirational. Is it wasting my time or educating me? Well, the lead singer is a great person who raises money for charitable causes so that is good. It

probably isn't educational but it makes my mood feel good so it has to be a positive thing really. The star now has full approval.

Role Models.
We have talked about celebrities but role models may often be people that you know. Study your role models and see what makes them successful. You will find that 99.9% (perhaps even 100%) of them worked very hard to be where there are today so have a look at their habits and life lessons.

Remember This Is Your Life With Your Name On It!
You cannot be your role model! Remember, they own their life too. Perhaps you can be like them by studying their success habits.

Here's how – a little challenge…
It is easy to look at people that are in your hero status locker but look at other successful people too. Perhaps a friend, colleague or a friend's parent is successful too. What made them successful? Maybe a teacher or neighbour recently told a personal story of how they did something that they were proud of. How did they achieve this?

Study people and listen to people who are full of wisdom, take their wisdom and bottle it for later. Hold on to these stories of real people and form patterns in your mind about their stories. Become a collector of stories, a collector of wisdom and you will notice good success habits to use in your own life.

Warning – some people aren't always the best role models.
Some people, famous or not, don't always tell the truth or they may display poor success habits. By studying as many people as you can, you will soon identify who they are though.

Milo paused and put his book down. He wrote the names of some friends' parents who seem successful, a couple of teachers' names and a handful of celebrities.

It was time to finish getting ready for school. As he packed the last few bits in his school bag, straightened his tie and popped his

jacket on, his eyes cast over the picture of the band. With a guitar in hand and a super-imposed band logo behind the other musicians on the print, Milo smiled to himself. "What a performer," he muttered to himself, "A hero of mine. One day perhaps I could play like that!" With that thought in his mind, he wandered down the stairs and headed out the door to school.

The school day was the same old, same old Monday. The Gorgeous Crew (as they called themselves) were constantly checking themselves in the reflection of the big glass windows. The Hard Nuts (which nobody admitted to calling them) were strutting around as if they owned the place. They thought they were intimidating but most people just ignored them or laughed quietly to themselves. Then there were the Stattos, a group of science-fiction fans who knew every quote about every sci-fi film. They were in deep discussion about quantum physics or something. Neil the Eel was wandering around groups of people trying to sell something. He was called that because he wore lots of gel in his hair and everyone thought he was a slippery character. He would always buy something off of someone and try and sell it to someone else at a profit, a great business idea but he was never usually successful in making the sale.

Lessons and more lessons followed plus the usual conversations between students about stuff. You know, stuff? To Milo's delight, the day seemed to fly by for a Monday and it was soon time to go home.

He climbed aboard the bus; he was off to meet up with a friend on the other side of town. Two ladies in their thirties sat on the seat facing him and they were deep in conversation, talking loudly about their favourite celebrity gossip.

"Oh, did you see Celebrities on the Deserted Paradise Island last night?"

"Yeah," replied one of the girls, "I want to be Suzy Cute, she's amazing. She has the perfect figure and she's so talented. That is soooo me!"

"Yeah and when she had a go at Micky Abs and put him in his place. That showed him didn't it?"

"And I reckon Golden Gary will get voted out soon, he's such an idiot. Can't stand him. He cheated on Sandy Sandie!"

Milo turned his nose up as he looked out of the window and watched the traffic building up on the opposite side of the road. The two break from their chatter, one was scrolling through her mobile phone and the other was glancing at a celebrity magazine.

"Oh my God, have you heard that Famous Freddie from Fortune Grows in My Moneybox has been done for drink driving? He cheated on his girlfriend last month and they're gonna split up but she announced she's pregnant as well. Don't think it's his baby anyway though."

"Nooooo, I never knew she was pregnant. I mean she's been seeing another guy too, hasn't she? I hope she gets what's coming to her."

Milo smiled to himself, conscious that the ladies may look up and catch him at any point, so he covered his mouth with his hand and continued to listen to them pass their opinions on these celebs, people that they didn't know personally. He wasn't really into celeb gossip, that was his sister's speciality and it irritated him.

The truth is, you can change and become a different person by changing your habits but none of us can do the old trick of Clark Kent, walk into a phone box and become Superman by magic.

Firstly, define why you want to change who you are. Maybe you have a bad habit that is holding you back and it needs improving. Perhaps it is a confidence issue and you need to create a new self-belief. You must ensure it is a deep-rooted reason and not just a shallow, passing phase.

An example of the latter could be because everyone else is doing it and you feel that you should fit in. Peer pressure is dangerous at times. It could also be some media influence telling you that everyone should be doing this or suchlike.

Remember that celebrities still get up in the morning, eat breakfast, brush their teeth, work hard through the day, pay their bills, have families, have pressure, feel happy and feel sad. They do all the things that we do too.

Beauty Is Not Airbrushed.
Ever picked up a glossy magazine and seen that perfect supermodel with seemingly beautiful skin with not one blemish on it? Her hair is amazing and not one strand is out of place. With a sleek figure, her clothes hug the contours of her body. Then there is the guy with the six pack abs, tanned skin and muscles on show. His hair is similar in perfection and skin totally conditioned. Inside the magazine will be a subtly placed advert on how you can supposedly achieve the same by buying some amazing products.

Would you like to know their secret? Well here it is:
Shock horror, it is called digital enhancement! All you need is a computer and some sophisticated software. You knew that, though didn't you? Yes, you can achieve that by pressing a button on a device in the palm of your hand. There are various apps and photo enhancing software packages readily available to change your image within seconds.

Beauty versus happiness.
Sadly, various recent studies show that people, especially teenagers are more obsessed with their appearance and what others think of them than they are with seeking happiness. They would rather hide behind an image than actually go free and enjoy themselves. It is a myth that stardom, fame and money will equal happiness. Proof is in the numerous stories of well-known stars checking into rehab, suffering mental-health problems or even worse, committing suicide.

Go back to nature, natural is beautiful.
Go to any natural beauty spot on our lovely planet and you will find that most have been created by natural sources.

Go and see the world, it is an amazing place. Take in the beauty! Our travels have taken us to beautiful beaches in Asia, Europe, Africa and more. Sardinia is one of the most amazingly unspoilt places we have seen, as are some of the islands in the Andaman Sea, Thailand, the dramatic rocks on the Italian coastline and the Greek Islands plus the African countryside. There are too many places to mention. Closer to home is the New Forest in Dorset, the dramatic Yorkshire countryside and stunningly rugged Devon and Cornwall coastlines plus the pretty villages and farmlands in our home county of Northamptonshire.

The Seven Natural Wonders of the world are The Northern Lights, Great Barrier Reef, Mount Everest, Grand Canyon, Paricutin Volcano, Victoria Falls and the Rio De Janeiro Harbour.

Are these airbrushed? No!

Are their dimensions in perfect measurement? No!

Do they have any slight imperfections? Yes!

Are they rugged and slightly (if not) well worn? Yes indeed!

Are they air brushed for our pleasure? Absolutely not!

Nobody decided one day to rebuild the Grand Canyon because it wasn't the right shape or change the colour of The Northern Lights because they liked pink instead that day.

Nature is amazing and some of the most amazing phenomenon on our planet was created naturally. Watch a David Attenborough documentary if you are unsure. These awesome wonders of the world were created over millions of years not by the click of a button so why should we be any different?

Sadly, too many people are hooked in by society's influence and they lose their own inner and outer beauty.

Take pride in your appearance.
We certainly should take pride in our appearance of course. Always be clean, it costs next to nothing to look after your hygiene. Dress smart and wear appropriate clothing. There will be times when you are judged on your appearance (as the world will judge you). Wearing a suit for an interview for instance.

Simple advice:
- You are who you are, you have inner beauty.
- Take pride in your appearance, simple and straightforward.
- Celebrities do not really look like that.
- A smile is nicer than a pout.

One of my former students was a very attractive young lady who had just turned twenty. She worked on a perfume/make up counter in a local retail outlet and was a smiley, happy person with an infectious personality and brilliant communication skills. In fact, it would be a challenge to find anything not to like about her.

She wanted a change of career and found a job through our organisation with our support, and to be fair, she didn't need much as she was a natural. This led her onto a business-related apprenticeship where she attended our college every week.

One day she arrived for her morning training and she looked different. Some of us trainers and other students commented at how nice she looked that day but she played it down a little. In fact, she seemed a little embarrassed with our usual compliments that we used to give when credit was due.

There was something we couldn't quite put our finger on this day though. Why did she look different and what had changed? Her smile was there, she was smartly dressed as always and full of her usual positive, chatty personality.

Suddenly a female trainer commented, "You haven't got any make up on today." Now the chaps hadn't noticed and our female colleague said this a little louder than the young lady would have liked. Suddenly she became conscious and hid away from the centre of attention as the other students turned to have a look.

"I know, I can't believe I forgot this morning. I have never, ever forgotten to put my make up on but today for some reason I did," was her reply.

Everyone commented on how much the lack of make-up suited her. She felt a little self-conscious and hoped that nobody would notice but suddenly everyone was throwing her some amazing complimentary comments.

A few of use pleaded with her to try this "new look" again but she didn't want to at first.

Now I am going to leave that story there because this young lady's story mirrors that of many girls that we used to meet through this organisation. Some would tone down the make-up and some would cut it out altogether. Some would be too scared to change the comfort blanket they found from the daily application of foundation etc.

Now if you are a lad reading this then you may think that you have an easy ride and this doesn't apply to you. OK, maybe you don't wear make-up (of if you do I never judge – see the section on prejudgement) but blokes can be very vain too.

Ooh, now to tread carefully, we all have a certain amount of vanity in ourselves but the bottom line is, we are who we are and we need to be proud of who we are.

Be yourself, everyone else is taken.
Think about who you really want to be and be yourself, not the airbrushed model. If you are not 100% with something, change the things you can change.

Your inner beauty will cascade outwards. If you feel great on the inside then it will be infectious on the outside.

Beauty attracts beauty but only natural beauty will win.

Be your best self and people will love you for it.

Nobody will ever be 100% satisfied with everything but create your own belief.

Airbrush is fleeting and beauty is ever lasting.

But remember, you are you and be proud of you!

Milo's Toolbox:
"I am Milo and this is my life!"
Does it matter what other people really think of me if I believe in myself?
How do I move away from life pressures such as, you must look like this, own this, wear this or not be laughed at?

Milo Challenges You:
Think about you and who you are.

Make a list of your real qualities.

Remember there are rules in life. For example, school tells you what time to be there, what time to go to the toilet, what time to have a break and what time to go home. Some jobs do this too and the media society conditions us to be what they want us to believe.

Who are the influences in your daily life? People close to you and people in the media, celebs etc.

Consider, are they positive or negative?

Real or fiction? Realistic or make believe?

Could you emulate them? Would you really want to emulate them?

Do they add value to your life?

Also, imagine that you were to move 200 miles away from where you live to a place where you know nobody. The majority of people in your life right now, you would lose touch with a massive amount of them within a year. You would become a distant memory to them and they would to you. Now, does it matter if you have perfect hair or have the latest designer label on your clothes just because others do?

What type of person do you want to be? Kind, respectful, likeable? Now list the qualities that you would like to possess and we can look at how to work on these later.

Fun Facts – Are you a copycat or do you suffer from CWS?
Your life is your life but some people do have the desire to be someone else. Elvis Presley is the most impersonated celebrity in the world. From tribute acts singing his songs to imitation Elvises conducting wedding ceremonies all over the world. Arnold Schwarzenegger and Jack Nicholson are the second and third most popular to be imitated.

Celeb-obsession.
Do you suffer from CWS? That is Celebrity Worship Syndrome, a recently identified psychological condition. It is believed that one in three people are so obsessed with someone in the public eye that the obsession affects their daily life. Psychologists at the University of Leicester say that the number of sufferers with some form of CWS, or mad icon disease, is going up. Time to avoid the celeb magazines at the checkout!

X is for X-Rated – Honesty is the Best Policy

"Honesty is the first chapter of the book wisdom." – Thomas Jefferson (Third president of the USA)

Milo got home that evening, did his homework and ate his tea. It was time now for a bit of a reward, so on went the television. He popped his feet up on the footstool as he slouched comfortably into the sofa with a fluffy cushion propping his side up.

"Ah, this is the life!" he said, as his parents glanced up at the television screen.

"What are you watching?" his mum enquired, as Milo flicked through the channels.

He came across one of his favourite programmes called Lily the Looter's Virtual Crime World, which featured the criminal underworld. The main character was a good-looking chap who, in the opening scene, was driving a car away from the law in a high-speed pursuit. His sidekick, Lily the Looter, was leaning out of the window, firing bullets from a pistol at the pursuing cars. The car gave the police the slip as it turned into a side street and screeched to a halt. The driver hopped out and opened the boot to reveal a man who was tied up, hands behind his back with gaffer tape over his mouth. The tape was ripped off in one move and a few low-blow punches were delivered to the man's stomach before he was hauled from the boot and thrown to the ground. Lily the Looter climbed out of the car and pointed the pistol at the man's head and some words were exchanged about drugs, money and a rival boss who they were trying to track down.

The family were now engrossed in the programme, catching up on where the last episode had left the story. Time flashed by and before long, the closing credits were being shown and it was almost time for bed.

"I can't believe I've just wasted an hour of my life watching that rubbish," said Thea, his sister.

"Yeah it was pretty naff," agreed Dad, "All good entertainment though!"

As a debate broke out between them, Milo said his goodnights and headed upstairs to bed. After cleaning his teeth and cramming a few bits into his school bag, he thought about his body clock for a moment. There was still a little time before he needed to switch the lights out so he decided now was the time to commit to his Future Toolbox. After sending a couple of social media posts, he picked up his book and opened it at the next chapter entitled "X-Rated".

Milo's eyes widen. X-rated normally meant something a little controversial, sometimes perhaps relating to something rude, so he read on.

Is it legal?
The world is obsessed with illegal acts and heinous, dreadful crimes. Switch on the TV and you will find endless shows glamorising the murky underworld, drug lords, sex, violence and godfathers.

Wow, thought Milo, as he remembered the TV show he had just watched. It was almost as if this book had been watching him watch TV.

With the big Hollywood screens bashing out box office classics, actors do a great job. They make car chases speeding through cities, dodging bullets and breaking the law look a whole lot of fun. It is easy to see how cool the Don or the Godfather is.

We can all enjoy a good film whilst munching our popcorn at the cinema, dreaming the dream of being the bad guy. You know, the one that sits behind a big desk in a mansion, handing out orders while throwing endless supplies of money around at expensive things. Sometimes we know how wrong it is but it looks like an amazing lifestyle. The male character is surrounded by loads of girls and the female character always gets the hunks falling at her feet.

Sadly, this is impressionable to all of us but it can influence our choices for later in life.

Behind the bike sheds.
"Go on, just try it… just one… chicken…" Perhaps you have heard those words from your friends.

Just one cigarette, one sip of alcohol or even worse, drugs!

These things are illegal!

Some people may argue that cigarettes and alcohol aren't illegal but they certainly are for an under eighteen-year-old.

Many poor choices can lead to an addiction which could lead to serious life consequences. We are all the sum total of all of our life choices:

- Smoking – if used as intended over a period of time, cigarettes have a high chance of killing you!
- Alcohol – long term misuse will affect your ability to function and contributes to long-term adverse health effects!
- Drugs – instant high but long-term low. Soft drugs can lead to hard drugs and hard drugs can lead to all sorts of bad places!

Those are just short statements of what these poor choices could result in – so think before you start.

An easy survey! Ask 100 smokers if they would like to quit smoking. And then ask them if they regret taking up smoking. Most of them will say they wished they hadn't started.

Think before you make a choice. Think about all those X-rated things that may look really cool on television and ask if that is the choice for you.

Remember, just like we talked about in **Y is for Your Life**, television also isn't necessarily real.

Milo thought of a couple of the Hard Nuts Crew who smoke. They're always hiding around the bike sheds and sneaking in a cigarette at break times. Some time ago, one of the group offered Milo one but he refused because he doesn't like the smell. He remembered being pressurised and made fun of because he refused, they started calling him names too which was a little intimidating. One of the friends did try a drag on a cigarette and immediately started coughing.

A family member smokes and the ashtray on the coffee table looks disgusting when it's full.

As he popped the book on the floor, his mind started to wander about the Lily the Looter in the TV show. He thought of the driver and began to think how unreal and made up this was. It was really entertaining and sometimes he wanted to be that person in that film or show. It all looked so cool but they are all probably going to end up in prison or getting shot.

Of course, most of us are respectable people that know not to break the law but sometimes we try and crack the system. **Rules are rules** whether we like them or even agree with them however, we have to respect them.

For example, it is illegal to break the speed limit in a car but many people do it. When they get caught, some drivers will not accept a fine and maybe blame the police for making money, challenge the limit in the area they were caught or credit their own ability as a driver at speed. Ask a driver how good their driving is and the majority will tell you that they are brilliant.

It is also illegal to drop litter but sadly too many do with little regard to the environment. How many people drop chewing gum or cigarette ends for instance, and they think this is perfectly OK?

Milo thought about the school rules and how many students broke them. He and his best friend Rico used to see how long they could get away without wearing their blazer inside the school building – a school rule. Why did they do that, he wondered? Neither of them particularly liked their school uniform but there was little point in not wearing it inside the school because it would only get them into trouble.

They also once got into big trouble when Rico suggested they skipped school but they got caught by a teacher who was out on a dentist appointment and they ended up in detention. Milo chuckled to himself thinking about their crime attempt that went wrong.

Milo also broke one of his mum's favourite vases recently. He was messing around with a few friends and he threw a ball to one of

them in the house, sending the vase crashing to the floor. They buried the evidence at the end of the garden and he played ignorant to what happened to the missing ornament. His mum was a little upset but more confused about what had happened and knew either he or his sister were lying.

"Now that was the perfect crime," he thought to himself, trying to justify his actions. His mum knew that it was one of them and still regularly mentioned it hoping for the truth one day.

Many friends were always late for school and lessons or hanging around in restricted areas and so on. This would result in consequences.

However, he wasn't really interested in breaking the law and being in trouble with the police. That was a problem for one of the family friends who was caught drink-driving last year. The driver was over the limit and was stopped by the police, arrested and charged. This resulted in him losing his driving license as well as losing his job. The friend messed up his career and had to work in a low-paid job, which meant he couldn't afford a family holiday that year.

He also knew of a neighbour who ruined their life by regularly taking drugs. The addiction got so bad they lost their job and ended up committing fraud. This led to a criminal record and they eventually lost their home and had to move away. The last the family heard was this neighbour was still really struggling with life.

Cheats never prosper!
Surely you have heard that phrase many times before but it is very true. My family brought me up with this phrase, they taught me to **always be honest** and not to lie. My mum used to say, "To lie, you need to have a good memory!" Lying is too hard so I just found it easier to tell the truth in the end.

Lying, cheating and dishonesty are probably the worst things people can do to each other… you wouldn't want to be on the receiving end of this.

When I was at school, I used to copy my friend's homework. He was a good mate and got me out of trouble many times. One day he said to me, "Mark, you really need to do this yourself as you will never pass your exams." Trouble is, I didn't like homework and it was easier to copy.

So that would probably be classed as cheating and ultimately, I ended up being behind on my coursework and didn't make the grade in some of the exams. My maths teacher insisted that I spend an extra three evenings a week with her after school to catch up, this wasn't the most enjoyable experience of my school life.

Cheats do get found out in the end and my results and performance found me out by not doing my own homework. I would now never recommend copying a friend in school, just copy their habits but not their work.

OK, I tried to cheat the system and most of the time the system will win but it is really lying and deceit that people cannot stand. Our world should work on an honesty policy and the more honest you are as a person, the more respect you will receive. Sadly, the more people lie the more they start to convince themselves that this is the truth in their own head. Then they probably spend more time working on the lie instead of being up front. Honesty is always the best policy, be honest with yourself and honest with others. It is a path to gain the respect you deserve.

As I said, I gave up trying to lie, it is easier to tell the truth.

Milo's Toolbox:
Be legal. Breaking the law will only get you into trouble. Be careful of getting in with the wrong crowd and being influenced by the wrong people.

Tell the truth about the broken vase and offer to buy a new one·

Milo Challenges You:
Now we don't want to know how illegal you have been here, what crimes you may be hiding. Hopefully that will be a little joke but a serious question, have you ever lied when it is actually easier to tell the truth?

We all make mistakes, that's why pencils have erasers. However, is there a time where you weren't entirely honest with someone recently? Perhaps you blame someone else or told a small lie to cover something up.

Milo challenges you to be honest and own up. Go and tell that person the truth and apologise to them. You will get so much respect and it will ease your conscience.

Fun Facts – Scams – Catch me if you can
Popcorn in cinema costs £4 to buy and 7p to produce and how much does it cost to make a cup of coffee? Some people would call that a scam! The price of popcorn and coffee for instance, all legal. Though what about con artist, Frank Abagnale who wrote fraudulent cheques worth more than $2.5 million in twenty-six countries in the 1960s. You may recognise his name from the blockbuster film *Catch Me If You Can* where Leonardo DiCaprio played his character.

He moved to New York and made his only stream of income a number of scams involving banks where he made over $40,000 before running away. It wasn't just about money though, Abagnale travelled around the world free by pretending to be a Pan Am pilot, worked as a medical supervisor, a lawyer and a teacher until he was caught and put in prison for twelve months. After a successful escape whilst travelling to the United States, he was finally given twelve years in prison.

Yep, he managed to escape again but was once again captured in New York City and returned to jail. After serving only five years of his sentence, the US Federal Government gave him his freedom in return for helping the government against fraud and scam artists without pay. He currently runs Abagnale and Associates, a financial fraud consultancy company and is a multi-millionaire. The film may be an exciting watch but in reality, he wasted a lot of his life running and being in prison.

Abagnale may have broken an obvious law but in some countries, you may get into trouble without realising. Here's some of the silliest laws from around the world:

Here in the UK, we have some strange laws. It is illegal to enter the Houses of Parliament in a suit of armour and you would also be breaking the law if you died in there. Imagine being thrown in prison for dying.

Our nation is proud of royalty so it's an act of treason to place a postage stamp bearing the British monarch upside-down. Also, if the head of a dead whale is found on the British coast, it automatically becomes the property of the King, and the tail, property of the Queen. I bet they would be delighted. In Scotland, if someone knocks on your door and needs to use your toilet, you must let them enter.

Going across the pond to the States, it is illegal to get a fish drunk in Ohio and in Alabama, it is illegal to be blindfolded while driving a vehicle. This must actually be a pretty good law wouldn't you think? In Florida, unmarried women who parachute on a Sunday could be jailed and in Chicago, if a place is on fire, it's against the law to eat there. You better leave before the last slice of pizza. In Florida, it is illegal to pass wind in a public place after 6 p.m. on Thursdays.

In other countries, visit France and you can't name a pig Napoleon, chewing gum is illegal in Singapore and you are not allowed to flush the toilet after 10 p.m. in Switzerland. You get fined for running out of petrol on Germany's autobahn and hiking The Alps naked is illegal.

A question for you. How many Australians does it take to change a light bulb? Answer, one but only if they are a qualified electrician. Yes, you have to be a qualified electrician to be allowed to change a light bulb in Victoria, Australia. If you break this law, then you have to decide if it is worth the penalty. Apparently, rebels who defy this law could receive a fine of up to AU$10 (£5.50). How much does an electrician charge?

W is for Wonga – Becoming Money Literate

"Financial peace isn't the acquisition of stuff. It's learning to live on less than you make." – Dave Ramsey (international best-selling author and radio host)

During free study time at school, **Milo** picked up his book to take on the next chapter of his Future Toolbox. **This one looked exciting... talking about money. His friends at school would always talk of being millionaires and dream of driving fast cars, living in big houses by the beach and owning expensive worldly possessions.**

His parents were sensible with money and always taught him not to waste it but his aunt and uncle were always arguing about not having enough of it. He scanned to the first line of the page and was faced with a question...

Question: **"Do you love money?"**
Some people will say yes and some, believe it or not, will say no.
- I love money because it can buy me nice things.
- I don't like money because money is the root of all evil.
- The more money you have, the more successful you are.
- Millionaires are always happy because they have loads of money.
- Money is like oxygen; you need it to live.
- I would rather be happy than rich.

Above are some statements that can be heard when the subject of money is raised but whatever your attitude towards money is, we have to face some facts – we need it to live but the earlier in life we understand **financial literacy**, the richer we will become.

"Literate! Isn't that something to do with reading?" Milo thought to himself.

Literacy normally means being able to read but imagine being able to **read money** from an early age. To become money literate, we'll start in simple terms, as we could write a whole book on the subject.

It is painful to say it but **financial literacy** is a subject that isn't taught in the school curriculum but is probably one of the most important life skills ever. Students would have a huge head-start in life if there were regular lessons on money management, so we're going to start here.

The Misconceptions of Money.
There is a belief that you need to be a millionaire to be successful and happy. Not true – there are many unhappy millionaires. Some people have lots of money but no time to dedicate to their lives.

Studies show that the most successful people in the world are the ones who live just below their means. Those who spend less than they earn. If someone earns one million pounds in a year and spends two million, they are not successful, are they? If they spend half a million then maybe they are. The people who are the most aware of their spend and careful with their cash will enjoy success but enjoyment and generosity also come into play.

The story of the miser.

A man with a huge bank balance could afford to live a comfortable lifestyle. Sadly, he was really tight with money and rarely went out of the house. He had very few friends and people who came into contact with him were usually greeted with a scowl. He was dirty and so was his modest, terraced house. He was loaded but had nothing.

This person had little satisfaction in his life and went on to be very lonely indeed. All the money in the world could not buy him happiness because he would not allow himself to move away from his obsession with not spending money. Is that a good way to live? Erm, no!

The story of the Sir Spend-a-lot.

One of our students, a teenage worker got paid weekly, every Friday. He would go to the pub and celebrate payday, the weekend. Woohoo. He would also pay back his parents the money he had borrowed the previous week and then live it up on Saturday. On Sunday he would borrow some money off his parents to put petrol in his car and then throughout the week for similar essentials, until Friday would come around again. Yep, the same scenario would occur.

This person is living on credit or loans and this is unsustainable in the long term. The spender lives from payday to payday and is currently battling to stay even. In the short term, it may be enjoyable but the day arrived where he could not afford to make the next step in life. He struggled to become a homeowner, experience luxuries and be free from financial worries because he was constantly paying off the next debt. He eventually became bankrupt.

The story of the super-saver.

Another student who was paid a grant of £30 a week in cash every Friday would immediately transfer three pounds into a savings account. Other students would laugh at him but he would proudly show off his bank balance as it grew slowly. He would say, "If I can save three pounds out of my thirty, then imagine how good I will be at investing money when I am earning mega bucks?"

He was a shrewd young man who went on to be really successful in his career and is now living a great lifestyle from investments. This all came from his early respect for money. It doesn't matter how small or large the amount, he started a savings habit.

Milo thought long and hard about the three people in the examples above. He had a piggy bank and his mum would make him put some coins in it every time he received money from family at birthdays or special occasions or even as a treat. Sometimes this was really hard, as he would see his friends buying the latest gadgets, games, clothes and suchlike where he did not always splash out his cash and make impulse purchases. He would still waste some money on treats like snacks, magazine and games.

And how much money did they spend at Father Russmuss's Food Box? It was a great place to hang out and chat but they would always end up spending money on food or drinks, sometimes they never really actually wanted to eat, they just did it out of habit.

Wall Street Waz, one of his friend's dads, was some kind of investor and drove a really flash car. They went on expensive family holidays and his daughter always had expensive designer clothes. She would show them off at school sometimes and mention names like Armani, Christian Dior and Gucci. Everyone seemed quite impressed. Her dad was away with work quite a lot but when he was around and the group of friends went to her house, he always seemed very serious and not always friendly and welcoming. The daughter used to say how busy her dad was all the time and she never used to see him much, which was hard, plus he would always be busy answering phone calls and doing lots of work in his home office. A lot of the school students called her the "rich girl" and some were jealous and some were a bit nasty at times but she was always hardworking and a high achiever.

Milo started to imagine what it would be like to be rich. Everyone at school talked about being rich a lot but how do you get rich?

Ways to Become Rich.

It is fascinating talking to young people and hearing of ideas of how they think you can become rich. A popular way is to get paid for doing absolutely nothing. Nice try but let us know when you have found someone who will pay you for that idea. Here are some other popular ideas:

1. Marry someone rich.

   Perhaps, but a long shot. To attract someone filthy rich, you would need to hang out with filthy rich people and then convince them to marry you and give you lots of money. Good luck if you choose this option but it is a long shot.

2. Rob a bank or do something else illegal.

   There was a recent article about a multi-million pound bank heist that took seven years to plan, the robbers got caught and were given twenty-two years in prison. If you don't get caught the first time, you will always be on the run. We talked about X-rated illegal crimes in the last chapter – definitely choose another option.

3. Inherit or win a fortune.

   The odds of winning the National Lottery in Britain are fourteen million to one. Inheriting lots of money requires someone dying and leaving the money to you, assuming they have lots of money to leave you. Again, these are long shots or require something sad to happen to someone rich. Also, a recent study in the USA showed that seven out of eight lottery jackpot winners ended up broke within seven years. Half file for bankruptcy within four years and the suicide rate is three times higher than the national average. Perhaps instant fortune doesn't buy happiness.

4. Invest in a get rich quick scheme.

   Sounds good but these don't actually exist. The odds of getting rich quick are normally similar to the odds of winning the lottery. The best advice on get rich quick schemes, if something sounds too good to be true, then it usually is and is probably best avoided.

5. Generate a relatively high income from what you do for a living and invest a proportion of that on a regular basis. This could be a winner, as you would not be relying on someone else.
Option number five will lead you to something called **"financial freedom."**

There are two main types of income:

Linear Income – Time for Money.
You are paid for your time. If you earn £10 per hour and work ten hours, then you will receive £100. You stop working and you stop getting paid! Simple.

Passive Income.
This is sometimes called "royalty" or "residual" income and is where you earn money from something without having to repeatedly do some work. Ways of achieving this could be from:

Investments that pay an income – putting down capital (a large sum of money) into an investment, perhaps property, a bond or shares, for instance. Money is paid back in interest or income.
Royalties – this is where someone is paid over and over again for work they have done once – pop stars, authors, network marketing.

Assets versus Liabilities.
It is good to understand that assets make you money and liabilities cost you money.

A mobile phone or a brand-new car is a liability, because it is unlikely that you will ever be able to recoup your money from it, as it depreciates in value. For example, when you buy a new car, it automatically loses value the minute you drive it. It is unlikely to ever be worth anywhere near as much again in the future.

Property or stocks can be assets, as they can be bought and generally increase in value. They can also decrease though and that is called financial risk.

Please note – a lot of investments are normally more successful long term and some carry risks of losing as well as making money. For example, stocks and shares can go down and even go bust altogether. This is where you really need to go and talk to a fully qualified and trusted financial adviser for more information.

"Aha, Wall Street Waz is always talking about investments, stocks, shares and property income," Milo thought to himself. He had no idea what these things meant but had heard mention of them in films on TV.

He started to think more about money and how he earned it. His parents gave him and Thea money each week for doing jobs around the house such as cleaning the car, cutting the grass, doing the washing up and keeping their rooms tidy, for instance. The more jobs they did, the more money they would receive as their allowance.

Aha, linear income, Milo thought to himself, swapping time for money. He then thought about what he did with the money and realised that he spent it on things like snacks, magazines and games. Hmm, these are not assets. He peered around his room and realised that all of his possessions were not assets, as he could not realistically sell them for more money than they cost new. The money his mum made him put in the piggy bank could be invested.

"Hmm, stocks and shares perhaps," he thought to himself chuckling. "At the moment, more of my money helps to make Father Russmuss and his fried chicken shop richer."

Thea was a lot more disciplined with her saving. She would save more of her money until she wanted to buy something specific. She would put as much money as she could into her piggy bank each week. It was usually small change but it added up over time and their dad would sit with her and count up the pennies before they made a trip to the bank to deposit it into her junior savings account.

46

Milo was less excited by doing this; he wanted to spend his money now but his dad would always say that he wished he would save, like his sister. Perhaps he should start to think about putting some change into his bank account.

Work to learn, not to earn.
In the early days of anyone's career, they need to build up experience. Be keen and find out where your role fits into the process of a company.

A waiter or waitress is responsible for taking food orders from customers and providing front-line service. If there is a complaint, then it is their responsibility to resolve the complaint and make the customer happy. This employee needs to understand that perhaps a message needs to be relayed back to the kitchen staff and let the chef responsible know that the food order was not to the customer's satisfaction. Perhaps the food needs replacing. This in turn will hopefully solve the customer's issue and the waiter/waitress has to show empathy and be polite to reach this outcome. Why?

A satisfactory outcome will mean the customer will hopefully return to the restaurant and spend more money there. More money spent will result in higher profits for the restaurant and ultimately more success.

This is not to mention the tips that waiting staff can earn too. Of course, not every job will give tips but the knowledge you could learn could be worth much more in the long term.

The long-term learning here is the skill of customer service, how to work as a team, how to deal with an objection or handle a situation that was not caused by the person in question and the purpose of that person's role within the profitability of a business.

"Formal education will make you a living; self-education will make you a fortune." – Jim Rohn (entrepreneur, author and motivational speaker)

Milo enjoyed reading about money and realised that he now had a better understanding of why he should start saving. He picked up

his journal and tapped the end of his pen on his bottom lip whilst in thought. His parents would pay him up to ten pounds for doing all the chores and sometimes he would skip a few of them and get five or six pounds.

Now he was a little more grown up, he decided that he wanted to get a part-time job and start earning some good money. An application form for a local coffee shop sat on his desk waiting to be filled in. Perhaps that would be a good time to start saving a little more.

Milo's Toolbox:
Do all of my jobs around the house to earn as much money as I can.
Apply for the job at the coffee shop.
I can learn something as well as earning money... learn how to be a bit more organised.
Put together a savings plan. If I can earn ten pounds every week, then I can save one pound of that money and still have more than I had before.

Milo re-read the notes he had written and smiled to himself. It sounded so simple that he could not believe he had never worked this out before. Perhaps this was his first step to becoming rich.

Milo Challenges You:
Look at what money you have coming in (income) and how much you spend (expenditure).

Start by looking at how much money you earn and make a note of it. Write down to the penny, the weekly or monthly figure. It doesn't matter how much or little you earn.

Look at how much you spend on a weekly or monthly basis.

Do you have regular bills such as mobile phone (and rent etc if you're a little older and paying them – remember this book is for all ages and so are the exercises).

On the list, are there any things that you're paying for that you could cancel? Erm, no… you can't cancel the rent, that is essential. Do you pay for a magazine subscription that you don't really read? How about a gym membership for a gym that you don't visit? Cancel it or even better, start using it.

Now the next bit is powerful, but it needs two things: honesty and effort.

Take a small notebook and write down every penny you spend for thirty days. Yes, every penny. That means every time you go to a shop and buy a bottle of water, a snack, a coffee or a magazine. Include everything to clothes and major purchases. Maybe it will surprise you how much money you waste… we all spend without realising how much it adds up to.

Finally, is your income more than your expenditure? If yes, this is good and if no, then you are living beyond your means and need to change something drastically.

Fun Facts – Is this wasted wonga?
Some people just spend, spend, spend. Billionaire Russian oil tycoon Roman Abramovich bought a 405-foot yacht worth $168 million on eBay, the most expensive item ever purchased on the popular online marketplace.

Other crazy buys have included: Lunch with Warren Buffett – $2.6 million, a house with a war-proof bunker – $2.1 million, a town in California called Bridgeville – $1.77 million and even a guy called Ian Usher sold his life – $309,292.

Think that is weird? How about spending $28k on a grilled cheese sandwich that supposedly has the face of the Virgin Mary on it? People have sold items like a "ghost in a jar," a "possessed" rubber duck and even the "meaning of life," the latter only fetched $3.26 in 2000.

We talked about celebrity obsession before but a Britney Spears fan spent $14k to buy a chewing gum spat out by the star during a concert in 2000. Another idiot spent $1,025 on Justin Timberlake's half-eaten sandwich. That is just plain stupid!

V is for Vegetables –
A Healthy Body and a Healthy Mind

"Garbage in, garbage out." – George Fuechsel (early IBM programmer and instructor)

Thursday came and went at school, another day of lessons, a bit of revision for some exams and some dramas thrown in. One of the Gorgeous Crew members bought a mobile phone from Neil the Eel only to find out it didn't work. He refused to give a money-back guarantee and ended up in trouble. One of the Hard Nuts was drafted in to chase him around for the whole day until he offered a full refund. This all seemed to slip under the radar of the teachers though so it only ended up being Neil the Eel's pride that was damaged.

At home, Milo picked up his book for his next Future Toolbox **lesson and immediately turned his nose up when seeing the chapter title – vegetables. Urgh, he thought to himself... a plate of greens did not excite him. As he munched his way through a bag of crisps, he sighed, took a deep breath and read on.**

An apple a day keeps the doctor away – proverb.
This old proverb is believed to date back to the 1860s in Wales. The original wording of the saying was, "Eat an apple on going to bed, and you'll keep the doctor from earning his bread." This means eating an apple full of vitamins and minerals is likely to keep you healthy.

Perhaps if you are not convinced, try completing this phrase instead:

A cheeseburger a day...

Ha, you cannot say, "Keeps the doctor away" and seriously expect it to make sense, can you?

Milo chuckled to himself and said aloud, "Good point!"

He looked at his packet of salt and vinegar crisps and pushed them to one side for a moment. Picking up the book, he looked left and right quickly to make sure nobody was looking before sneaking another crisp into his mouth and read on.

"A pizza a day..."
"A can of cola a day..."
"A takeaway a day..."

None of these phrases work with the ancient proverb, do they? So how do we stay away from these seemingly tempting and tasty convenience foods and snacks?

"The doctor of the future will no longer treat the human frame with drugs, but rather will cure and prevent disease with nutrition." – Thomas Edison (inventor and businessman)

Firstly, if you buy a meal from a fast food restaurant (please note, these outlets sometimes use the words meal and restaurant to make them sound more appealing), the "meal" from the "restaurant" usually contains empty carbohydrates, saturated fats and added sugars, which are all processed ingredients.

When these components hit your body, your body thinks, *"Ooh, what is this? I am not sure what to do with this so I will store it over here for now!"* Your body will store the fat in the junk cupboard.

Next, the little engine in your body will look for some fuel from your energy store to perform a task but it will have to search high and low until it finds something in the junk cupboard.

Your brain is getting mentally stressed and is wasting excess energy whilst looking for extra fuel. Your body is trying to function on but is low in energy. Your performance is affected because you are now being run on junk fuel – it is a little like pouring sand into the petrol tank of a Ferrari.

Poor fuel is like throwing a piece of tissue paper on to a fire – it will burn quickly. A thick, chunky log will burn for longer and therefore is good fuel and this is what we need to put into our bodies.

A piece of tissue on the fire diet – you will crash and burn.
Short-term effects mean you feel low in energy and your performance in tasks will be low. You will feel tired quickly, possibly stressed and have trouble concentrating.
Long-term effects mean that your immune system will take a nosedive and you could (and probably will) get colds, bugs and feel poorly easier. Longer term, this could lead to adverse health effects including risk of serious illness and diseases.

A log on the fire diet – eating proper food will maximise your potential to function.

The energy drink option.
Many people reach for the products that claim to "give you wings" or turn you into a "rock star" or "monster," so to speak. These fizzy drinks are heavily loaded with sugars or chemical equivalents or are caffeine-processed products that will inject a dangerous lightning bolt of false energy into your body.

Warning, warning – sounds cool but not fun. Repeat... not fun!
Getting struck by lightning or sticking your fingers into a plug socket is dangerous! A processed energy drink or bottle of fizzy pop will do the same.

OK, it may not kill you like an electric shock could but it is not good for you. Some of these products contain a third to a half of processed sugars. Your body will spike in energy and put it in the junk cupboard and the cycle will start again.

Milo stared at the almost empty packet of crisps on the table and tried to understand that something so tasty could be going into his junk cupboard. Picking up a crisp, he held it up to the light and examined it. This piece of potato certainly did not look like the vegetable that it once was, making it obvious that it was processed.

Get your five a day.
According to the NHS, evidence shows there are significant health benefits to getting at least five 80g portions of fruit and vegetables every day. Some countries even recommend seven portions.

"Eat your veg" was usually the topic of conversation at the dinner table during meal times, as his parents tried to get Milo and Thea to get their "five a day."

Through his t-shirt, Milo patted his tummy, he certainly was not overweight. He was active at school and enjoyed sport but then he suddenly remembered that in PE, he sometimes felt a little light-headed. Perhaps this is something to do with the "tissue food" fuelling him, he thought to himself.

A girl in his class was always worrying about her weight and would not eat much, talking about calories all the time. She would look at pictures of celebrities in glossy magazines and bore everyone in earshot about being a model. Another boy was the opposite – he ate crisps, chocolate and snacks all the time and could easily drink a huge bottle of fizzy energy drinks in a morning, even though the school had banned them. It all seemed very confusing.

It can be a minefield knowing what to eat at times but things do not have to be too complicated.

If the food is grown naturally then it is usually good.

If it is processed, then nature has been tampered with. Think about the following:

Are chemicals added?
Good foods will go mouldy more quickly than processed foods.

Are there any added sugars?
Giveaways: if it is sweeter than it should be or sauce has been added.

Does it contain words like "concentrate"?
Look at the first ingredients. If they contain something ending in "ose" – glucose, sucrose, dextrose, fructose – this is added sugar. It is worth noting that fruits are naturally sweet though.

Does the food look similar to when it was grown?
If no, it has probably been processed. Generally, anything that comes in a packet (instant meals, ready-made meals etc.) is processed.

Is it in pill or potion form?
Pills, supplements and shots aren't good enough to replace real food. Like anything, there are no short cuts in life.

Top tips.
1. Your body needs a balanced diet to live – eat properly.

2. Be careful of clever marketing from companies trying to sell you products.
3. Put good food into your body and you will get good results. The opposite is – garbage in, garbage out.
4. Processed foods are usually easy to spot – if they come in a packet, they are probably not fresh.
5. Eat five to seven portions of fresh fruit and vegetables a day.

So, does an apple a day really keep the doctor away? Well, apples contain high levels of acetylcholine. Erm what's that exactly? It's an organic chemical that functions in the brain and body of humans and animals. As a neurotransmitter, a chemical message released by nerve cells to send signals to other cells which helps increase movement and sensory perception. In simple terms, that means making you more mobile and helping your brain to function. Some studies have even shown that apples also reduce anxiety.

Guess what, no burger, pizza or kebab has shown these results if eaten on a daily basis.

Your brain uses 20% of all **glucose**, 35% of all **vitamins and minerals**, 40% of all **water**, and a staggering 50% of **good fats** in our bodies. Time to put the good stuff into your body, here are some great suggestions of what to eat to stimulate the brain and keep healthy:

- **Nuts** are packed with **nutrients and good fats** and filled with **nature's energy**. Go for natural, unsalted nuts though, dry roasted peanuts don't count.
- **Blueberries** contain more antioxidants in a single blueberry than any single supplement and show the ability to hugely improve memory, verbal comprehension, decision making, and numerical ability. Want to get better at maths, eat blueberries.
- **Turmeric**, that yellow stuff found in curries, is a super little anti-oxidant that has been shown to help just about everything from fatigue to major diseases. The Alzheimer's Society has acknowledged claims that turmeric has helped sufferers although there is no real evidence to support it as a treatment.
- **Pumpkin Seeds** are not just leftovers from Halloween, they contain several good fats that are important for brain health.

Also, during stressful times, we use more zinc in our bodies (especially men). Pumpkin seeds give you have a fast replacement which triggers stress release.

- **Broccoli** has been shown to be one of the best foods after a traumatic brain injury. However, you don't need to have suffered an injury to benefit from the several nutrients in broccoli that surround and protect new neuro-connections in the brain, helping things to move from short-term memory to long-term memory very quickly. In fact, any dark leafy greens are a must.

- **Dark Chocolate**, now we're talking! The darker the chocolate, the richer it is in fibre, iron and magnesium, which all help the brain receive blood flow. It also contains natural caffeine that is way better than coffee and those terrible energy drinks. All in moderation though.

There you have it, a short list of good food to eat. Notice that there isn't a single processed food, pill, or artificial ingredient. We don't need to know how it all works or exactly how much you need, the simple advice is, go healthy and eat in moderation. The worst foods are generally anything packaged. If it's in a package, it's not food, it's a food-product. It's a subtle difference, we can eat food-products, we just can't get nutrition out of them. Processed means less energy for you.

Oh, and don't forget to drink plenty of water, staying hydrated means your brain works more effectively. It's the best energy drink you can have.

Milo thought about his diet for a moment. He scribbled in his journal a list of foods that he ate regularly and put a tick against what he thought were good and a cross against those that were not so good. Biscuits, sweets and fizzy drinks got a cross and carrots, potatoes and onions got a tick. Ones he was unsure of got a question mark to find out more about later.

Trying to give up all of the ones with crosses would be too difficult surely, but he knew that some small changes would be a good start.

Milo's Toolbox:

I am going to commit to replace sugary drinks with water from now on and only drink fizzy drinks once a week.

I will cut out fast food and snacks once a week to start with and instead of eating sweets every day, I will replace them with a piece of fruit. Treats are OK now and again but I'll be more aware of what I eat. Sorry Father Russmuss, perhaps I'll have to order more healthy food now.

Milo Challenges You:
Diet is important so Milo urges you to spend a lot of time on this.
- Step 1: Be aware but not obsessed with your diet.
- Step 2: Rate your diet on a scale of one to ten (ten being amazing) by looking at the portions of healthy versus unhealthy foodstuffs you consume daily.
- Step 3: Look at minor improvements such as replacing one snack or drink at a time on a daily/weekly basis.

Fun Facts – Aeroplane food maybe?
Whilst we know that fast food pizzas are fattening and vegetables are full of goodness, we are not entirely sure about the nutritional value of an aeroplane. That's right, those things that fly in the sky!
Well, French entertainer Michel Lotito knew all about this.

His favourite delicacy appears to be bicycles as he ate eighteen of them in his time, but his most astonishing accomplishment was eating an entire light aircraft in just over two years. It does say light aircraft so perhaps the calories content is lower than a jumbo jet.

U is for "U Can Do It" – Silence the "I Can't"

"Whether you think you can or you think you can't, you're right!" – Henry Ford (founder of the Ford Motor Company)

Silence the "I can't" and build the "I can".
"I can't" and "I can" only actually have a small difference in appearance. The difference is a few letters – "not" or "t" if you abbreviate. Yet this small difference makes a huge impact on your end result. Turn the negative statement into a positive belief.

If we look at Henry Ford's quote: "Whether you think you can or you think you can't, you're right!" If you think you can do it then you will

believe in it but if you think you can't then chances are, you **won't**. Build the belief slowly. If you can't do it yet, then find out how to.

Yay it's Friday, woohoo. Everyone had a spring in their step as the knowledge that the weekend was only around the corner lifted everyone into good spirits. After the first lessons, Mrs Lombardi asked Milo how his Future Toolbox was going. It had been a whole week since he had been handed the book and begun reading.

"Very good, Miss, it has been really good fun and useful. I have read something every day and have been writing in my journal," he said, proudly patting the book.

Suddenly, one of his other teachers, Oli Switchblade, entered the room. Mr Switchblade, or Sir to the students, always came across as a really scary man who could really put the fear into you. You certainly didn't want to cross him or get into trouble that he knew about. His voice was loud and his eyes were piercing and you could hear his footsteps clumping down the corridor. Even some of the Hard Nuts stepped into line when he was around.

Thumping his pile of books and folders onto the desk at the front of the class, he bellowed "Morning Milo."

"Errr, morning Sir... how's... how are you?"

"Good... in fact, very good!" Mr Switchblade always repeated things to confirm that you had heard them.

Fidelma wandered into the room as Mrs Lombardi had asked her to pop by at breaktime and chat about how things were going with her Future Toolbox journey. She wasn't particularly affected by Mr Switchblade's presence in the room, she sort of floated in and said, "Hey everyone! Miss, Sir, Milo!" Pulling up a chair, she popped her bag on the floor and sat down, leaning her chin on her hand waiting for someone to ask her something. Milo couldn't believe that she wasn't scared of this man, the one that made your heart race faster every time your paths met.

The Future Toolbox had been posting tips on social media and Mr Switchblade mentioned that he had been reading them throughout the week. The teachers then suggested that they all have a look at the next chapter together. Milo was thinking that he wanted to hang out with his mates as it was a nice day outside and the school field looked so much more inviting than the classroom.

Milo was first to speak and he opened his mouth and said, "I can't Sir, I have to..." he then paused for a moment.

Stuck with no real excuse, he looked at Mr Switchblade and then at Mrs Lombardi and immediately changed his mind. If his teachers were kind enough to help him then why not take up the offer? Fidelma also agreed. If truth would have it, saying no to Mr Switchblade without a good reason could spell trouble in his eyes.

"Ah it doesn't matter, I'll get my book and journal," he said, dropping his bag on the desk and pulling up a chair. He took one last look at the sunshine out of the window as everyone hung out on the field. Fidelma sat next to Mrs Lombardi, who leaned over the desk, slid open the drawer and pulled out her copy of the book. Mr Switchblade opened his briefcase, pulled out his books and joined them on the table.

"You can do it," Fidelma read aloud and then joked about the clever use of the "U" for "You". "I will have to teach this guy to spell," she continued, looking at Mrs Lombardi. Their teacher was always picking the students up on using slang in English. She read on,

How many times have you said the words, "I can't" recently?

It is probably on a daily basis. Sadly, people are very good at saying "I can't," before they have even given the task any thought whatsoever.

What does "I can't" mean?

There are normally two reasons for saying "I can't".

1. You do not have the confidence or belief that you can do it.
2. Saying "I can't" actually means "I won't".

Number 1 is called a limiting belief and number 2 is also usually the result of a limiting belief.

DANGER – A limiting belief will stop you in your tracks. It will halt your progress by slamming the brakes on very hard!

This also applies to "I don't know," which is an easy and lame phrase used to just close the mind. The brain becomes lazy and human nature sometimes uses this to avoid thinking.

Making the change.
How do we change the "I can't" into "**I can**," the "I won't" into "**I will**" and the "I don't know" into "**I do know?**"
All are similar.

The first step is to build your confidence and belief to overcome your limiting belief. This is done by changing the way we think. This can be done by simply changing your language.

Start by thinking of something you can't do and write down the following, filling in the blanks:

Milo picked up his journal and thought of something he says he can't do all the time. He wrote down the following:
- **"I can't do maths!"**
- **"I can't do maths yet."**
- **"I am getting better at maths."**
- **"I am learning maths."**

He looked up at the teachers and said, "Ah, I get it, the first step is changing your language. Sir, Miss, what can't you do?"

Fidelma and Milo both leaned forward in anticipation, knowing they had put their teachers on the spot, and awaited their response.

Mr Switchblade looked at Mrs Lombardi and scratched the back of his neck. He had announced in class last week about his quest for fitness and, after a short pause, said, "I can't do press ups!"

As he said this aloud, he picked up his pen and wrote these words in his journal and as quick as a flash, Milo piped up with step two.

"Erm, OK, Sir, you said you cannot do press ups but now you need to remove the limiting belief by using positive language. It is time to change your negative to a positive!"

Mr Switchblade then wrote,
- "I can't do press ups yet."
- "I am going to get better at press ups."
- "I am going to speak to Mr Gymfit, the PE Teacher, and learn how to do press ups."

Milo and Fidelma were now reading from the same book and Fidelma added, "Now we are going to look at your limiting belief, Sir, and we are going to try to remove it." She smiled at Milo as the pair now started to feel like the teachers. "Could you do one press up, Mr Switchblade?"

Their teacher looked surprised and replied, "I guess I could, I have done them before, yes I could."

Milo looked at Fidelma and asked the next question as he read from the book, "Sir, if I asked you to do 100 press ups now, the chances are that you would not be able to. However, if I asked you to do one or two, do you think you could do them?"

Mr Switchblade stood up, took off his jacket and smiled. As he sheepishly looked around the room to make sure nobody had snuck in to watch, he moved to a space in the classroom. Taking a deep breath, he put his hands on the floor and did two full, complete press ups. Smiling as he got back to his feet, dusting his hands together, Milo, Fidelma and Mrs Lombardi clapped his simple achievement.

"So there you go Sir, you have now removed your limiting belief and proven that you CAN do press ups," Fidelma said proudly. "You can now say…" the four of them called out together, "I am getting better at press ups!"

Milo then went on to explain from the book that if Mr Switchblade could do two press ups, then he could probably do three, four or even five in one go. His teacher agreed and, after initially saying no because he was not dressed in his gym kit, Milo and Fidelma convinced him to do five press ups.

"OK Sir, now you have proven that you can do it, you could easily do five press ups again in one hour's time."

Agreeing, his teacher realised that he could actually do 100 press ups. All he needed to do was repeat five press ups twenty times over a day or so. Realising how powerful this simple concept was, Mr Switchblade committed to doing 100 press ups over the next couple of days and said he would report back to everyone after the weekend. At that moment, the bell sounded for the end of the break and everyone scribbled a few notes in their journals before going their separate ways to their next lessons.

Milo walked down the corridor with his head held high. Feeling good that he had helped his teacher and worked with another student that he was getting to know better, the value of life skills was really starting to pay off. What's more, he realised that Mr Switchblade was actually a decent person not just a scary teacher. Who would have thought that he would be getting this so-called scary figure to drop on the floor and give him press ups? It was almost like something an army colonel would get his cadets to do as part of a training routine. Sometimes we prejudge someone before we get to know them properly.

Training our brain to get what we want, not what we don't want.
Our brain is split between the **conscious** and **subconscious**, one gives the orders and the other obeys. Although the **conscious** tells the

subconscious what to do, the **subconscious** is the most powerful and will always follow the strongest command.

The easiest way to explain this is to think of a television. On the screen you can see an image of a programme. Imagine you want to change the channel, what do you do? That's right, you hit a button on the remote control. You hitting the button is now the **conscious command** which will send a signal to the television telling it to change the channel.

What happens next in a millisecond is quite remarkable but we take it for granted. The remote control sends an infrared signal from its receiver to the television receiver. The television receiver activates some kind of microchip which sets off a chain of events in the electrical circuit commanding the channel to change. A new beam of light appears on your screen and a new channel appears with a different visual and a different sound. This is like the **subconscious command** working. In a millisecond, thousands of things have happened to change the channel on the TV but all you did was press a button and noticed an instant change without thinking about it.

Your **conscious** mind can process around five to seven things at once but the **subconscious** can handle millions.

So, the great thing here is to now train our mind to get what we want and avoid what we don't want. That sounds simple but how do we do that?

As a child, we experience many positives and negatives. When we learn to walk our parents normally say something, "Well done, that's brilliant, you're taking your first few steps. Now keep going, keep going... oops you fell over..." They will heap words of encouragement onto you as you walk, fall, get up, fall again, cry, crawl, have a cuddle, try again and eventually master this.

However, there are also some negatives. "Don't touch that, don't shout, don't run, don't talk to strangers and don't stay out later..."

Now these bits of advice may be in your interest of learning and will keep you safe but they all begin with "DON'T!"

Focus on Positive Thinking.
Firstly, let us talk about focus. Have you ever seen a photographer with one of those sophisticated cameras with a focus button on them? You know, the ones where they have to turn the lens to get the picture in focus otherwise the picture is a blurry mess?

Well that is the first step. We need a focus, a target or a goal.

Next it needs to be the right focus. For example, at exam time we need to be focussing on...? At a job interview... a sports event... You can fill in the blanks...

Next focus on **what you want**, not what you don't want.
Don't think of a pink elephant with pink fluffy ears and a big pink trunk.

What are you thinking about? Ha, pink elephants? If you're not, you either fibbing to me or you're not focussing on this book properly.

We have to focus on what we want **not** what we don't want.

Ever been walking down the street and your mate says to you, "Oh no, it's so and so over the road, **don't** look?" What do you do? Yep look!

You're watching a scary film with the same friend and they say, "Arghh, the next bit is really scary and gruesome, whatever you do, **don't** watch it!" You know it, you're going to watch.

You're in class at school or maybe in a meeting at work and somebody walks past the window. The teacher or leader of the meeting says, "Don't worry about that person outside, don't look out of the window!" Suddenly everyone turns to look out of the window.

"Say this and not that!" Your mind focusses on "That!"

"Don't forget your pen/keys/glasses/briefcase/wallet/purse!" Now your focus is on "Forget the pen/keys/glasses/briefcase/wallet/purse!"

Your subconscious will follow the strongest command so make it a positive one. If you ask people what they want from life, you sometimes get responses like, "I don't want to fail my exams; I don't want to lose my job; I don't want to put on weight; I don't want to be skint" and so on. Their focus is on what they don't want and not what they do want!

"What do you want in life?"

"Well I know what I want. I don't want to be broke, I don't want to lose my job and I definitely don't want to fail my exam. That would be a nightmare. I don't want to be fat and I definitely don't want to break out in spots!"

What is this person focussing on? Negative wishes.

They don't want to lose their job so what happens. There are redundancies at work and they are fearful. They put pressure on themselves and their work performance starts to suffer. They are ratty with their colleagues at work and then the boss has to make a decision. "Sorry son, your performance is not up to scratch so we're offering you redundancy." Arghhh, now they get run down and break out into spots!

"I don't want to fail my exam!"

Relax, step back and refocus… look at the bigger picture. **What do you want? What is your focus?**

Let's try this example – "I will pass my exam" or even better, "I have passed my exam". Now your focus is on **what you want!**

Watch world class athletes on the TV lining up for the 100 metres. What are they focussing on? What's for tea? I must watch the telly at 8 p.m.? Don't forget to pick up a pint of milk?

Nope, it's winning the race (just in case you hadn't guess the answer, of course).

Let's now get rid of the negative thoughts. These are called limiting beliefs and there are some examples below:

Limiting Beliefs.
- I'm too young/old.
- It's too hard to...
- I'm not smart enough.
- I'm not good enough.
- I'm rubbish at...
- I'm so unlucky.
- I'm too busy/don't have enough time.

You know what to do, change your language and focus on what you want not what you don't want. You are more likely to be successful.

- Instead of saying, "Don't be late," say **"Make sure you're early or on time!"**
- Instead of saying, "Don't forget your keys," say **"Remember your keys!"**
- Instead of saying, "Don't look down," say **"Focus ahead or look up!"**

Milo's Toolbox:
Don't underestimate my own abilities.
Silence the "I can't".
Open my mind to solutions.
Focus on what I want and not what I don't want, use positive language.

Mr Switchblade is actually not that scary.

Milo Challenges You:
Milo says, recall something that you have said "I can't" to recently and think of a way where you could have said "I can".

Cut down the use of the phrases, "I can't," "I won't" and "I don't know!"

When presented with a task, pause for a moment before giving a negative answer and seek a solution.
Using positive language, write a list of things that you want in life.

Fun Facts – Can you beat Oli Switchblade?
Well Oli Switchblade has just discovered that he can do press-ups after all but he still has a long way to go to catch Japanese world record holder Minoru Yoshida. In 1980, he managed an amazing 10,507 press-ups non-stop. Yep, he could do it!

T is for Time – Tick Tock Tick Tock

"If you love life, don't waste time, for time is what life is made up of."
– Bruce Lee (martial artist and movie star)

We all have exactly the same number of seconds, minutes and hours in the day. Guess what? We also have the same number of days in a week or a month and the same number of days and months in a year. Time passes at the same rate for everyone. Bizarrely though, young people seem to feel that a week can be a lifetime and older people feel that time rushes by at a scary rate. When you are bored, time drags and when you are having fun, it flies by.

"Every day is a bank account, and time is no currency. No one is rich, no one is poor, we've got twenty-four hours each." – Christopher Rice (American author)

The key to time, though, is what you do with it. Human beings tend to waste it with mindless and invaluable acts or with poor planning. **Time is the greatest gift!**

After another busy weekend, Monday morning soon came around. Milo was reading the next chapter of his Future Toolbox **book whilst eating his healthy breakfast. He felt a little more alert this morning and started to credit that to his body clock now getting used to its new routine of going to bed a little earlier. When the alarm had sounded, he almost leapt out of bed thinking about all the things he could do that day after his "can do attitude" session with his teachers and Fidelma on Friday.**

His mum was rushing around as normal, trying to get her things together for work and his dad was shouting up to Thea who was still in her room.

"Does that girl take longer and longer to get ready each day? She'll make me late again. Now where are my keys, has anyone seen my keys? I CAN'T FIND MY CAR KEYS," he shouted, as he began to get a little irritated.

Milo chuckled to himself, as this was a daily occurrence around the family household in the mornings. He looked up from his book as his dad rushed past but thought better of giving him a lecture on changing the "I can't" find my keys to "I can". The timing was not quite appropriate as his dad threw down his jacket onto the chair and fumbled down the side of the cushions in a fluster.

Milo noted in his journal – Dad can't find his keys… turn into "I can…" He could maybe chat to him later.

His parents were extremely proud of him for taking part in the Future Toolbox **programme but had not really had the time to chat**

much about it yet. It was as if everyone got up, rushed around whilst eating breakfast, went off to school and work, came home, had dinner, rushed around again before watching television and then went off to bed. Milo took another spoonful of fruit from his breakfast, sipped his water and continued reading.

Quality Time.
How is it that some people seem to get lots done and others struggle? Why are the busy ones more successful than those who have little going on? Yes, we all have the same minutes in a day but let us look at how we may be spending them.

Feeding your Mind.
No this is not about eating, it is about the time you spend on the education to entertainment. In **V is for Vegetables,** we talked about diet. The stuff we put into our body in the form of food and drink affects us physically and mentally but the same concept applies to what we put into our minds. I heard a phrase called the E to E Diet which stands for Entertainment versus Education.

Entertainment.
OK, there is nothing wrong with entertainment; in fact, we need our minds to be stimulated by something fun and engaging. Watching *Lily the Looter's Virtual Crime World* and other TV shows is similar to junk food, fine in moderation but not in excess.

Education.
You may be thinking... oh no, school is boring... lessons... exams... tests...! This is not necessarily what we are talking about here though. Education, experience... these are things that will help us grow as a person.

Your E to E Diet Plan.
A little exercise for you – make a note of how much time you spend in the next day (or week, if you can) on the following:
- Social media (including chatting or messaging friends).
- Watching television or streaming videos.

- Playing games (consoles/apps/computers).
- Reading material (books/magazines/newspapers).

Then make a column next to these titles and split how much was entertainment and how much was educational.

Be honest right now…
Entertainment versus education:
- A cat falling off a lampshade in an online video, a dog running into a window or a guy falling off a bike in a hilarious manner – these are all entertaining (although not for those starring in the videos) but are they *really* educational?
- Sending, receiving and enhancing selfies of you and your friends is probably great in the moment but will it enhance your knowledge of life?
- Completing the next level on a game, even that one that has taken you attempt after attempt is hardly going to make you a success and will be forgotten as the next game is released.
- Reality television, celebrity gossip magazines and blockbuster movies have been talked about already earlier. Entertaining – perhaps. Real life – probably not. Educational – debatable.

To make this exercise really powerful, track your habits over a week to see what you are putting into your E to E diet. Are you filling your mind with sensationalised media, fun but pointless entertainment or mindless information more than you are challenging your brain to grow?

Warning – A Shocking Statistic on Wasted Time.
How much time do you waste? Think about all these little gadgets: mobile phones, televisions, tablets, games consoles and so on. A recent survey showed that people are spending six hours a day glued to these little screens. SIX HOURS A DAY! This cannot be productive.

Perhaps read an inspirational book, watch a TV documentary that you can learn something from, talk to a friend about something you want to achieve in life and then discuss ideas about how you could achieve it or how about playing a quiz game where you have to answer questions or think quickly? These things will all stimulate the brain and will be good fun too.

Suddenly there was a crash, which made Milo sit up from his book. Swearing aloud, his dad had knocked over a vase on the table next to the sofa. He had found his keys between the two pieces of furniture but in his retrieval, the manoeuvre had gone horribly wrong and water was now dripping off the top of the table onto the carpet. Stress levels were rising in his mum's voice too as she picked the flowers up off the carpet and yelled up to Thea yet again. Noting the stress, Milo went to help but was feeling a little nervous, this may now open a whole new inquest over the last broken vase.

"Where has the time gone again this morning?" his mum asked. "Every day we seem to be running late!"

Click, click... his sister appeared from upstairs, tapping away on her mobile phone. The noise of the keys irritated their parents but they were pre-occupied in clearing up the last of the spillage. Next came an annoying loud sound of music from his sister's phone as a video started playing and she chuckled to herself, totally engaged in the screen. She easily beats six hours a day Milo thought to himself.

"I'm beginning to think that the phone is actually one of your body parts Thea," said Mum.

A few words of exchange went between mum, sister and then dad, as she appeared to have the phone glued to her hand. It was time for her lift to school so moments later, it was just Milo and his mum and all went a little quieter. Thankfully, it was enough to deflect things away from the broken vase incident so all would be good for the time being.

Still shocked at this statistic of wasted time on social media, Milo shared this with his mum who rolled her eyes in relation to his sister's habit. He thought about his own habits. Playing games, social media, television… he is a teenager of course so loves these things. He enjoyed some of the educational television documentaries that he watched with his dad who loves the science and nature of the planet but the drama shows on catch up probably would get a thumbs down. Milo committed to himself to make a note in his journal of his E to E diet plan for the next week to see how much time he actually spends on entertainment. It was time to head off to school now so he packed his book into his bag, said goodbye to his mum and headed out of the door.

Making a Plan.
Homework sucks! Well most people think so but it has to be done. Sometimes we put off the horrible and boring jobs for those that are fun. Adults do it, teens do it – it seems to be human nature. So let us make a plan on how to be effective with our time management.

Mr Switchblade took the register and then introduced the lesson plan for period one.

"Right, class, this morning we are going to look at time management. Time management will help all of you become effective when you come to do your homework and revision." A groan went around the class from some students but, un-phased by this, he continued, "As always, we are going to keep it simple and of course, fun!"

The teacher then paused as he picked up a book off the desk and Milo noticed it was his copy of Don't Get Your Neck Tattooed.

"Yo, Switch," called a student from the group of Hard Nuts, known for his smart but not very witty comments, "I'm finking of getting ma neck tattooed with my girl's name on it…"

He was soon pulled into order by the teacher who had heard it all before. The futile joker was warned and moved and Mr Switchblade continued to read the following steps from the book and wrote them on the board.

Step One.
"OK, step one, make a list of all things that you need to do. This, class, is called a "to do list", clever eh?"

Step Two.
"Put them into the relevant boxes in order of urgency:
- "Urgent – this task needs to be done pretty much immediately.
- "Non-urgent – this can wait a few days or even until next week.
- "Essential – it will have a consequence to my studies if not done.
- "Non-essential – it is not going to really affect my studies if not done yet."

Step Three.
"Use a planner or diary and enter in the things that happen every week such as school, a job, sports practice, hobby and such like. Next, slot in the tasks around the commitments that you already have. Think about how long each task will take to do."

Step Four
"Stick to the plan!"

The class spent some time in groups on each of the steps above and began making some simple study plans. Two students were completely sold on the process – Milo and Fidelma. They worked with friends in a group and found themselves taking charge of the table, helping to make sure everyone was engaged in their plans. Mr Switchblade hadn't asked them, they just used their initiative after seeing that the simple technique was endorsed by the programme that they were following. If it is good enough for successful people to make a simple plan, then it was good enough for them.

Future Toolbox

Milo's Toolbox:
Track how much time is spent on the E to E diet·
Make my "to do list" regularly and stick to it·
Talk to Dad and help him turn "I can't" in to "I can"·

Milo Challenges You:
Make a simple plan, it could be daily or weekly. Keep it simple.

Make a to do list and then number each task in order of importance.
1. Blank out your commitments (job/school/college).
2. Add in weekly events (sports practice/family events/weekly meetings).
3. Slot in the tasks from your to do list into the free slots. Consider how long each task will take too.
4. Tick off the tasks as you achieve them and review the plan on a daily basis.

Review your plan at midday and teatime and aim to complete 80% of the items on it each day.

Please note, there is something psychologically satisfying about ticking off a completed task. Our brain loves the sense of achievement.

Fun Facts – Time a-wasting
Time is there for us to cherish and we must value our freedom so being given a prison sentence would get in the way of doing what you want to do.

After being convicted for a long list of murders, assaults, rapes and kidnappings, a Florida serial killer called Bobbie Joe Long received one five-year sentence, four ninety-nine-year sentences, twenty-eight life sentences and one death sentence in 1985 – this worked out to be over 2,300 years. His surname Long certainly was quite fitting for the time he was going to spend inside.

That is nothing compared to Darron Bennalford Anderson, who was sentenced to 2,200 years for rape, robbery and kidnapping in Oklahoma in 1993. However, he appealed and after a new trial convicted him again, a few thousand years were added to his original sentence making the new total just over 11,000 years. After another appeal, he did get 500 years knocked off.

Nowadays we send an email or a text message that arrives in seconds but back in 1790, a letter was posted to a French town and arrived 220 years later. The reason, a small error on the address. The white envelope containing two sheets of writing paper was sent from Paris to the south-west-France town of Seix, near Toulouse. The sender put Saix, which was taken to the wrong sorting office 150 miles away, where it remained because the addressee could not be found. Bizarrely, it took a whole lot of paperwork to finally deliver the letter in 2010. All because of an 'a' instead of an 'e'. We hope it wasn't an urgent letter.

S is for Smile – The Laws of Attraction

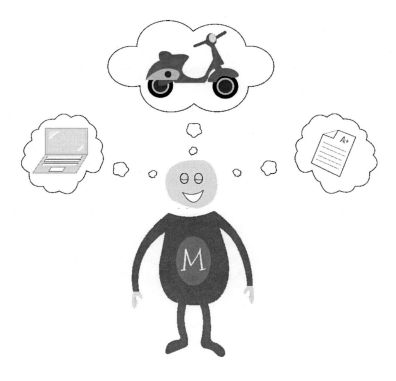

"Peace begins with a smile." – Mother Teresa (Nun and missionary)

Put a magnet next to a pin and the magnetic forces will pull the pin towards it until the two objects stick together.

Life is like a magnet.
Ever noticed that when you smile at someone, they generally tend to smile back? This is our **inner magnet** using a powerful force in life that goes a long way to influencing these outcomes. It is called **the law of attraction**.

Remembering a recent example, Milo had heard of the laws of attraction but wondered how it really worked.

His mum had talked for quite some time about owning a Mini. She went to the showroom to test drive one with him and his sister. They loved the small car and begged Dad to let their mum have one. The trouble was, they could not afford one yet but then something weird happened.

Every time they were out and about, they happened to see Minis driving around everywhere. It was as if someone had picked up a lot of these small cars and put them on the road or into every car park they visited. They even noticed that some of their school friends arrived at school in their parents' Mini. They went to a school fete and there was a competition to win a Mini on one of the stands. It even became a family competition to see who could spot the next Mini.

Mum and dad put together a savings plan and later that year, she finally bought a Mini from the showroom and is now happily driving it around.

So how did this happen? Coincidence? Perhaps not!

Activate Your RAS.
Your **reticular activating system** (or "**RAS**") is an **inbuilt radar** in your brain. This cool little device comes to life when stimulated and it is believed to play a role in many important functions, including sleep and waking, behavioural motivation, breathing, and the beating of the heart.

In the case of Milo's mum, her motivation was to own a car – a Mini. She thought about owning one and went to test drive it and then this car suddenly appeared on the road, everywhere she looked. Were the cars there already? Of course, they were! Nobody from the car dealership suddenly put them there to try and sell them to her; beep, beep, beep... the inbuilt **RAS** radar is on again and it detected the cars and made her aware of them.

Now she was noticing the cars everywhere, her desire to own a Mini rose and she began the process of bringing the laws of attraction into play. She thought about driving the car and focussed on what she wanted, similar to the positive thinking in the "**U Can Do It**" chapter. Her dream became a reality because of the RAS and Laws of Attraction working together, plus some defined goal-setting thrown into the pot.

Excitement began to build in Milo's mind as he thought about his dream car and a new gadget he wanted to own. These cars were evident on the streets in his mind and lots of people were using these gadgets everywhere. There is clearly more to the laws of attraction and being aware of my RAS, thought Milo to himself. Being realistic, he knew things did not happen by magic – of course there is a little bit of work involved too.

As Milo wandered home from school that evening, he noticed one of his neighbours walking the dog. The two of them made eye contact and Milo broke into a friendly smile. The neighbour smiled back as she passed and then said, "Hello." They had never spoken or interacted before but as they both continued on their journeys, Milo carried on smiling. The laws of attraction had come into play.

This was now turning into a fun challenge. As he opened the front door and walked into the house, Milo smiled at Thea. She looked a little confused at first but smiled back before going back to reading her trashy magazine.

Later that evening after doing his homework, the front door opened and Dad was home from work. Milo jumped up from his desk and walked down the stairs.

"Hey, Dad," he said, smiling. "Did you have a good day?"

"It was pretty good," he replied. "Wow, someone is in a good mood again, son. Looks like you had a good day."

At the dinner table, a family chat opened up and Milo pulled out his book and journal and introduced them to the Future Toolbox programme. Even his sister agreed to smile more around the house so all in all it was a great moment to share.

The laws of attraction brings a lady a dream home.
There is a lady I worked with and she moved to her dream home a few years ago. She could describe her ideal house right down to the final detail. In fact, we attended a goal-setting session and were instructed to draw a picture of our goals and she drew a simple drawing describing this dream home.

Now, at this stage, she didn't know where this house was or even if it physically existed. Amazingly, seven years later, her family moved to a detached house in a beautiful village. It had a winding drive up to the garage and a big, bold door in the middle. There was a tree on the left-hand side of the house and a lovely lawn at the front. It was what she referred to as the "house of her dreams".

Whilst unpacking some boxes, she found the picture of the house she had drawn back on that day. It was no work of art but it looked just like the "dream house" and she was now living in it. Her drawing even featured the tree on the left-hand side.

How on earth did this work?
We probably don't know how that worked but one thing is for sure – beep, beep, beep – the **laws of attraction** played a big part in this. If you want good things in life, then they will come but if you focus on the negatives, well the effect will be similar.

Another friend years ago used to talk and talk about emigrating to Australia. Beep, beep, beep – guess where she lives now?

One of my old students wanted to be a train driver at sixteen. Nobody took him seriously but he used to read about the train services and sometimes even read train timetables. Beep, beep, beep – no prizes for guessing what he does now.

Another guy wanted to be a pilot. Genuinely, not just for glamour. Beep, beep, beep – yep, he flies planes for fun now.

82

Of course, there is some work involved in actually achieving the dream, you can't just imagine having a brand-new car and then one will magically appear in front of your house the following day. Let's try something simple to get our **RAS** going. The next time you go to a busy place (say, the shopping centre or high street). As you walk through the crowd, wear a big smile on your face (not a cheesy one, go natural). Feel good about yourself and smile at other people who pass by. Please don't stare at these people and make them feel uncomfortable, simply smile if you make eye contact with them. Do the same thing if you are buying something from the checkout – smile at the cashier serving you and offer them a polite thank you for their service.

Now see how many people smile back at you. Not everyone will but this is likened to the **laws of attraction**. The more smiles you dish out, the more will come back to you.

When I started my first job at a building society, I chose to walk to and from work every day. It was two miles each way (yes, rain, shine, cold or hot, I would walk). On my way there or back, I would see the same people at various spots making their journey too. I would always smile and more often than not, they would smile back. After some time, I met a lady called Sue who would be power walking to keep fit, she would rush past some days. Bill actually worked in the same company as me and he was a train spotter who had a passion for steam engines. Then there was Bike Guy (didn't know his name) but one day when he fell off his bike, we made sure he was OK and a passing van driver gave him a lift home. He was always training for cycling events. Agnes had retired but carried on working at a little shop near town where she had been for over twenty years. She loved the customers there and wanted to carry on part time because it kept her active and gave her a little extra money so she could treat herself and her friends at bingo every week.

Why am I telling you all of this? This was when I was sixteen years old (a few years ago 😊) but I can still remember what these people look like and their stories. I used to walk home with Bill at times and, being honest with you, I had no interest in trainspotting but his passion for it was amazing. Sometimes a few minutes of conversation or a long-term friendship can be built on a few moments of smiling. It opens your mind to what makes the world turn and what makes people tick.

Now it is easy to smile so let us try a different **law of attraction** challenge. Think constantly of the things you desire and keep focussing on them. Please don't make it an obsession (see goal setting for how to do this). If you believe it, then you have a better chance of this happening. Trust me, it works.

OK now there is a catch here. You cannot focus on being a millionaire for a week or so and suddenly you wake up with an inflated bank balance. It isn't quite as simple as that but make your wishes and wants your focus and your instincts will start to follow.

The Magnet – Success Magnet.
Worldwide studies show that your lifestyles can be measured by the five people you spend the most time with.
Take money, people usually earn around the same as the five people they spend most time with.

If you hang around with **positive people** then you are like to be more positive. Spend time with those that moan then… well you know the outcome; you will become more cynical and negative about the world.

If you take school playground situation as an example. The students who play sport tend to be playing sport together. Those who like to study at break tend to hang out with study buddies. The musically talented spend time in the company of the musically talented. The trouble makers normally look for more trouble makers. The Gorgeous Crew hang out together, the Hard Nuts… the same.

Suppose you wanted to catch a cold. A simple common cold. Where would you go? Head for a group of people sneezing and coughing.

Right let's not talk about trouble makers or catching colds, those things are too negative but how do we attract the positives?

The first place to start is to look at your current social circle. Who are the people you spend the most time with? Who are they really?

Your best friend might be your best friend but they may also be leading you on a negative path. Are they distracting you from your goals? Do they step in your way when you try something different? Do they put you down and tell you that you won't achieve it, shouldn't achieve it or it is a stupid idea?

Now the suggestion here isn't to go and ditch your best friend and find someone else but it is to do a little social stock take.

Look at the positives in these people first and foremost. You clearly like these people so what do they bring to you? **What are their strengths?** What makes them tick?

It is important to think of your goals and not someone else's. These people will need to support you along the way after all. Tell them your desires and use their positive energy to propel you forward towards achievement and if a person steps in your way then sometimes honesty is the best policy.

If your best friend is the one who leads you down the wrong path then perhaps you could be the one who leads them along a more righteous one or being really blunt, if they hold you back that much, are they really someone you could call a friend?

When we set up our own business, we had a number of so-called friends who mocked our choice. Some of them wouldn't support it and would take every opportunity to make fun of what we were doing and to pass silly or even evil comments every time it was mentioned. One person would use social media to damage our reputation to the point where it became pointless even trying to justify our choice to them. How much time do you think we spend with these people now? Yep you guessed it – none!

Would it be better to hang around with successful buddies, people who are looking for similar things and maybe have already achieved some of the desires and wishes of ours?

So, if your life sucks a little, look at your circle of influence. Are they moaners or negative people? If so, make your informed choice and start advertising for new some new mates.

Of course, that last bit is tongue in cheek but it is time to evaluate the success of those around you and take that moment of control.

Successful people seem to enjoy continued success and if that is where you want to be, then focus on one thing... success. With some hard work and focus, the laws of attraction will be your friend.

Of course, you must work hard at these visions. Being blunt, you cannot live in a fantasy world that doesn't exist – the laws of attraction will only happen with focus (we will explore this later). Defined goal setting will help you achieve it.

Milo's Toolbox:
Smile. It makes me and others feel better.
The laws of attraction mean that the more I focus on something, the better the chances are of it happening.
Beep, beep, beep – activate my RAS to become more aware of what is around me.

Milo Challenges You:
The question from Milo is, if you want something, what do you have to become in order to achieve it?

Think about an example and then list the qualities that you require to become successful in achieving your goal.

Fun Facts – What are we attracted to?
Talking of attractions. It is amazing what people are drawn to.

Visitors flock to some of the weirdest tourist attractions every year. There is The World's Largest Chest of Drawers in High Point, North Carolina, USA. Fancy a trip to the Avanos Hair Museum in Avanos, Turkey to take a look at over 16,000 hair samples? If that's not your thing then there is stuff a bit closer to home. Try the only known Baked Bean Museum in the world in Port Talbot, Wales. Captain Beany set this up in his council flat back in 2005. By the way, we're not sure if Captain Beany is his real name.

If we haven't got you yet, we know you will be attracted to the Cumberland Pencil Museum in Keswick, Cumbria – no? OK, try the Abbey Pumping Station in Leicester. A real tour of excrement, sorry excitement... no it is excrement! In the nineteenth century this is where Leicester's sewage was pumped to be treated. Today its exhibits include the history of terminology for bodily waste written onto a toilet door and a loo with a see-through waste pipe so you can watch the progress of excrement "from flush to drain".

R is for Response-Ability – Your Ability to Respond

"The price of greatness is responsibility." – Winston Churchill (British Prime Minister)

"You two, get down here now!" shouted their dad in an angry voice.

Wandering downstairs, Milo was first at the scene of the crime, glancing a look at his father's stern face. Thea was a couple of steps behind and looking rather sheepish.

In a stressed and firm voice came the words, "OK, you need to take some responsibility and own up. There will be consequences!" The siblings looked at each other, then at the floor, wondering what they had done wrong and worse still, what the punishment was going to be should they confess.

"Who ate my last slice of cake?" Their dad broke into a smile and then burst out laughing at his supposed comedy moment. The siblings rolled their eyes as the giggling continued and eventually broke down into an occasional snigger.

"Yep, good one dad," said Thea in a pretty sarcastic voice. "You'll be a famous comedian one day."

"Fancy some TV?" Dad suggested to take away the awkwardness of his failed humorous attempt. "There's a cool documentary just starting. It's educational for you too, Milo," looking to gain approval from the E to E Diet in T is for Time.

Milo approved and the three of them popped themselves on the sofa and began watching the documentary about historical circus animals and how their owners trained them. The first story was about elephants; these huge but tame creatures would perform tricks in the big top and were rewarded with treats.

How to train an elephant.
Out in the wild, elephants are dangerous and ferocious creatures who could use their tonnes of weight to flatten anyone and anything in their paths; in fact, they could wipe out everyone in the circus tent in minutes. So how did the owners tame them?

From an early age, the circus folk would raise a baby elephant with a chain tied around its ankle. The other end would be attached to a small wooden stake and driven into the ground. As the elephant walked away from the stake, the chain would tighten and the creature would stop in its tracks.

Over the years, the elephant would grow bigger but its mind would remain conditioned that it could go no further than the length of chain. Every time it felt the pull on its ankle, it would stop when in reality, the stake would work free from the ground at a slight pull.

The story moved dramatically to the late 1800s where a fire broke out in a Barnum and Bailey Circus, people started running for their lives. The elephants reared up and bellowed in fear and pain but they could not pull the stakes from the ground and run to safety.

The programme ended temporarily for an advert break and the three family members, who had been engrossed in the story, began chatting. Milo talked of the Future Toolbox coaches telling this story in his school session the week before.

"People get stuck in a rut in their lives and are unable to break away from unhappiness or pressures that are thrown their way. They are like the elephants who could break free if they wanted to but can't work out how," he explained.

"Yeah, there's a chap I used to work with like that," replied Dad, "He moans about life all the time but never does anything about it. He does my head in!"

The programme restarted and they all fell silent again, becoming engaged in the next story which was called "How to Train a Flea."

Fleas have an incredible ability to jump from creature to creature in order to feed themselves and survive. If a human could jump this far, we would be able to leap around 100 metres from a standing position.

The story moved onto a flea circus from the olden days and showed how the hosts discovered how to train their fleas in order for them to perform small, intricate tricks. It was simple! A flea would be caught and placed into a small jar with the lid screwed on tightly. Every time the flea jumped, it would hit its head on the lid. After a few jumps, the flea would work out that it no longer wanted a headache so it would jump to within a millimetre of the lid. When the lid was taken off, the flea would never jump any higher again.

Milo was the first to speak excitedly when the programme finished. "Wow, we learned that we should not be like the flea or the elephants in this world. As mentioned before, people do get stuck in a rut like the elephant and not achieve their full potential like the flea. Sometimes we are presented with an opportunity but have a limiting belief and do not jump above the height of the jar."

Milo's dad was really impressed with his son's knowledge. "That is incredible. This stuff you have learned is really powerful – I think I need to read this book and chat to this mentor guy myself!"

"It is for everyone, Dad," Milo replied. "You know earlier you asked us to come and take responsibility for eating the cake? Well we were both scared of the word responsibility because it sounded scary but if you look at it differently, it is not so bad."

Milo then leaned over to the coffee table and picked up a magazine and a pen and scribbled on the blank space on the back cover.

Responsibility – The Ability to Respond.
He then ran upstairs, grabbed his Future Toolbox pack and ran back to his awaiting sister and dad, who were now staring at the words on the paper. He flipped open his book and started to read the relative paragraph:

RESPONSIBILITY may sound like a scary word but if you cut the word in half you have **response** and **ability**. Then change the order to **ABILITY TO RESPOND**, then this can lead you to success.

If we were to pop a chain on your leg and attach the other end to a piece of wood. Give you the key and then ask if you wanted to leave the room, would you leave the room?

Of course, I would!

Why, because you have the ability to respond. We wouldn't actually chain you to a stake in the ground but sometimes we let life chain us up and hold us back from seizing the day. Consider the following:

91

If an opportunity arises, then you have the *ability to respond* and either ignore it or take it.

If someone asks you to volunteer for something, then you have the *ability to respond* and either make an excuse or put yourself forward.

If you want to get fit but it is raining outdoors, then you have the *ability to respond* to your goal and either skip the workout and stay dry or head out into the rain and train.

If you are unhappy with something, then you have the *ability to respond* and carry on with the same painful process or to make some changes and start a new venture.

If you annoy someone or get into trouble, then you have the *ability to respond* and make an excuse or blame others or a circumstance or own up and take responsibility.

This process works for everything and everyone. We as humans are unlike animals. Animals can only live in the moment; they do not have the ability to set goals for the future and be anything other than creatures of habit. We have the ability to achieve our potential but so many people become pre-conditioned with their own limiting belief and accept being average or worse still, a failure.

Think about the challenges you face in your lives. Perhaps it is a big goal or event that is coming up in the future. It could be an exam, a job promotion, something that you are training for, auditioning for or competing for. Maybe it is a personal goal that you are trying to achieve or a benchmark goal that you have to make the grade at. It could even be a habit that you want to break or change.

If you think about what is required to achieve the above, then it will give you an idea of what RESPONSE-ABILITY you need to display to yourself in order to be successful.

It is all about **choice**! Do you choose to be successful or do you ignore it?

Milo stopped reading and looked up at his dad and Thea. They were both focussed on his words.

"Wow, Milo, I have never seen Thea listen to you for so long," he chuckled. "I can already see a change in your confidence since you mentioned this Future Box programme!"

Shooting him a bit of a look, "Future Toolbox," Thea corrected their dad, as she craned her neck to read the words from the back page.

They continued a conversation about the programme and the book and Milo's dad committed to making an effort to change some things that were stressing him out. He was always losing his keys and rushing around in the morning so he realised his *ability to* respond was to put the keys by the front door when he comes in the house. Simple!

Thea begrudgingly admitted that she spends too much time on her mobile phone, which distracts her from tidying her room and doing her studies. This makes Mum cross so her ability to respond was to do some of these tasks first, before getting distracted.

Milo had already started writing in his journal that his goal was to do better at Maths in school. He always skipped those extra Maths revision classes that were designed to help students who were finding the subject challenging, so his ability to respond was to take the opportunity.

Mum was working late again this evening and they all knew that she would be a little stressed when she came home because the project she was working on was taking up a lot of her time at the moment.

"OK, it is our ability to respond. Let us make sure the house is tidy and the dinner is all ready for Mum when she gets in," said Milo's sister, now fully in the spirit. "Perhaps we can chat to Mum and get her to think more about her new business venture that she keeps putting off, because she says she is a little scared. Maybe, this is the opportunity that she has the ability to respond to and take it on!"

The family began to rush around tidying, cooking and chatting whilst being productive in their chores. Mum arrived home to the lovely surprise of a clean house and a delicious meal. They all chatted around the table about their evening so far and the subject of the business venture was raised.

"I am quite excited, I have to admit," said Milo's mum. "It is a little scary because the money is good at work though. I tell you what, I will have another look at the opportunity this weekend when this week is over." She was now committed!

Milo's Toolbox:
I have the ability to respond to every task every day. This is my choice and as a human being, I have the choice to become successful.

Milo Challenges You:
- What did you eat?
- Who did you blame?
- What did you have the **ability to respond** to today?
- Did you take the opportunity or let it pass you by?

Think about the number of choices you have on a daily basis and you have the option to think of your response. Make a list and track your options.

Fun Facts – How would you like to take some responsibility?
If you do want some responsibility, get a job at one of the most guarded places on earth.

Fort Knox in Kentucky USA, is home to the US Bullion Depository, thousands of tons of gold are kept along with important historical documents. Just up the road in Nevada is Area 51, a top-secret aerospace development and testing site. It is believed that the area has hundreds of special sensors installed which can detect any movements in the area.

If you're not good at keeping secrets though, let's shout about these people responsible for saving millions of lives.

A man called James Harrison has magical blood. Yes, his blood contains a rare enzyme that can be used to treat babies dying of a disease called Rhesus disease. This unsung hero, Harrison, has donated his rare, life-saving blood more than 1,000 times over fifty-six years which has saved the lives of over two million babies around the world. Wow!

Others responsible for saving millions include Edward Jenner inventor of the smallpox vaccine, Jonas Salk, inventor of the polio vaccine and Alexander Fleming who discovered penicillin.

Q is for Quality – Be the Best You Can Be

"Why worry? If you've done the very best you can, worrying won't make it any better." – Walt Disney (Hollywood animator)

The alarm sounded and Milo groaned as he opened his eyes. His sleep pattern had been more regular, as had his eating, so usually he had more energy in the mornings. However, today was one of those nerve-wracking days. It was exam day!

There had been lots of pressure to revise lately and Milo had been getting a little overworked and anxious. A few of his classmates had given up long ago, including Rico, of course.

The two of them had been chatting on social media the night before. Rico said he had left his revision too late and he wasn't going to bother now. What was the point after all? He then realised that this was an error in his judgement and tried to cram-study, making his stress levels extra high. Milo had been trying his best to follow a revision plan that he felt was sort of working.

Wandering out of his bedroom, Milo met his mum on the landing. She looked focussed and was muttering some words to herself whilst shooting him a good morning smile.

"Hi, I've just started... no began a new venture... journey... business... erm... and I am would be delighted... erm... honoured... erm... be excited to invite you..."

After putting it off for quite some time, she had finally begun the part-time business venture that she had been considering and she was going to share the news with a room full of friends next week. She was practicing how she was going to speak to people to invite them to the big launch.

He was just about to shut the bathroom door but suddenly Mum called good morning to him. He paused, turned around and they swapped a quick exchange of the day ahead. The conclusion reached was, it was now or never. Preparation had been done – Milo had revised as much as he could and Mum was going to invite as many people as she could to give them as much notice as she could.

After getting ready, it was downstairs for breakfast time. Milo was soon joined by Thea. A healthy mix of fruit, muesli and yoghurt were on the menu today.

Thea was in a good mood this morning so he decided to share his plan for the day. The latest Future Toolbox advice had talked about doing your best in everything you do. As he opened the book he said,

"Hey Sis, listen to this…" and then he read from the chapter:

Be the Best You Can Be.
Firstly, you are an amazing and unique person. You may not realise it yet or even feel it, but you are.

Who Wants To Be A Success?
Who would like to be a successful person? I bet you are ready to call out, "Me, yes please! I want to be successful!"

"But I'm nothing special; surely I had to be born with a natural talent?"
Not true. If you research any successful person on this planet, you will find that nearly all of them started as a regular kid just like we did.

Albert Einstein was asked to leave school because his teachers thought he was "stupid" and Thomas Edison was classed as a "slow" learner at school.

There is a common theme with successful people in the spotlight – they all got to the top of their game. They ooze quality in whatever they do.

Now cast your mind back a few chapters. In **Y is for Your Life**, we looked at you and not someone else. Let's do the same with your qualities. It's time to **be the best** you can be.

Aim for **your** absolute best. Notice the word "**your**" was emphasised there?

Not everyone will finish in first place; it is impossible. Not everyone will score 100%… 100% of the time. Nobody will be completely perfect every time. However, if you have prepared well, it is time to now give it your best shot.

The biggest loser.
A great story comes from South Africa. The Comrades Marathon is the world's largest and oldest ultra-marathon race run over a distance of eighty-nine kilometres (about fifty-six miles). 20,000 competitors have

twelve hours to complete the event otherwise they are classed as a non-finisher.

It is reported that the first person who crosses the finish line after the twelve-hour limit receives a bigger cheer from the crowds than the actual winner. This competitor will not receive a medal or be officially recognised for their achievements but their effort is no less than the runner who finished in less than half the time they did.

This person was certainly **their best** on that day but certainly not the quickest, the fittest or even strongest maybe.

"Yeah but I've never been really great at anything…"
Oh yes you have! You just need to believe that you are good at things. In fact, there are lots of things you have achieved but you sometimes forget about them for one reason or another.

Perhaps we shouldn't always be as harsh on ourselves and our amazing achievements and accomplishments.

Pausing for a few more spoonfuls of his breakfast, Milo realised that Thea was completely engaged with the motivational script from the book.

"This sounds like something our drama teacher said in our competition last week," she said. "It was about doing our best and not worrying about winning the competition. As long as we tried our hardest and enjoyed it, the result didn't matter. We could feel so proud of ourselves and, even though we finished fourth, we walked away with our heads held high."

Milo agreed enthusiastically; he was really enjoying the new connection he seemed to be making with his sister over breakfast. Normally they wouldn't speak because they would be staring at a magazine or device or even disagreeing over something.

"Yeah, same for me in cross country. I never even come close to winning races but it's enjoyable and I give it my best effort. It's the

same thing really," he agreed. "Anyway, I'm gonna beat Dad in that 5K race in a few weeks ha!"

He smiled and continued to read aloud.

Remember, it is acceptable to try your hardest and not achieve but it is unacceptable not to try and fail.

Of course, you will feel disappointed if you pour your heart and soul into something and feel you have failed but you can be proud of the quality that you have displayed. This will also give you a platform for your next attempt, whether it is this task or something else.

Milo and Thea turned around and realised that Mum and Dad were standing at the door listening, both pleasantly surprised at the togetherness this little book seemed to be bringing to their family.

After overcoming their slight embarrassment, (remember, it's not always cool to impress your parents and like your brother or sister in public), they all agreed to be their best that day; Milo was going to try his hardest in the exam; Mum would call her friends for the business launch; Thea would give 100% in her drama practice; Dad had recently started a new running fitness programme and he would go a little further in time and distance. Milo didn't tell him he would beat him in the race in a few weeks though.

How big is your ego?
People sometimes complete to **be the best** just to make their egos bigger. The dictionary describes an ego as "a person's self-esteem or self-importance!" And some people try to be more important or bigger and better than someone else just to satisfy themselves.

Is it time to let it go?
Before our **Future Toolbox** days, we've worked with many people who have tried to overly justify their self-importance to the world.

"Oh, I'm the manager and you do what I say."

"I get paid more than you therefore I am better than you."
"I live in a bigger house, drive a faster car, paid more for my clothes and am just generally better than everyone so look at me!"

These types of people exist everywhere and sometimes it's an insecure way to live. It can come back and bite you if you are not careful too.

We had the pleasure of working with our local football team and some of the apprentices would use their opportunity within the sport to make their egos bigger. They were sometimes known as "The Big Time Charlies". Even some of the first team players wouldn't want to talk to the general public because they felt that they were too good and too important for this world. We won't name these people of course but thankfully they weren't the majority as most players at the club were decent and honest people who were doing something they loved. Many of the apprentices would be released at the end of their two-year time at the club as they hadn't made the grade and it was always eye-opening to see how the "Big Time Charlies" would react. Some would want our help and some wouldn't be able to cope as they had alienated themselves from everyone who had tried to support them on their journey.

Thankfully we know more rich and successful people from all professions (sports men and women, managers, business owners, directors, actors, lawyers, medics, dentists and rich, wealthy individuals) who are really decent people. In fact, one of the wealthiest people we know has a phrase and it's, "Get over yourself!" As soon as you accept yourself and can be yourself, your life will start to feel the balance.

The exam finished and Milo walked out of the room. Fidelma and her friend Molly caught up with him.

"How did you get on Milo?"

"Thank goodness that is over. It was OK, I know I could have done better with my revision but on the day, I gave it my best shot."

Molly said, "That is all you can do I suppose." Changing the subject, she added "Oh my, look at that. Who do they think they are?"

The Gorgeous Crew were all standing in a group, comparing their latest hairstyles and designer jackets, each one of them claiming that they looked better than the other. One was looking at himself in a pocket mirror and blowing kisses at himself. He heard Molly's comment and replied, "Hey Molly, where have you been all my life?"

"Ha, in your dreams!"

"C'mon baby, you know you love the Gorgeous Crew, we're not called that for nothing! You can come to our party at the weekend. I'll pick you up in my limo!"

Molly paused for a moment and looked him up and down, turned the corner of her mouth up and put her hand beneath her chin as if she was considering the offer for a moment.

"Erm… do you know what, guys… thanks for the offer but I'll have to say… erm… NO! After all, you'll need as much room in that big limo for your ego."

She turned and re-joined Milo and Fidelma as they made their way for lunch. The Gorgeous Crew weren't really that bothered by Molly's rejection but it made her feel her better by giving a polite no thank you.

"Anyway, who's hungry?" Fidelma asked.

Milo's Toolbox:
Be my best in everything I do, every single day·
Remove the pressure from myself to aim for perfect scores· If I try my hardest and don't succeed, then use this as a foundation to build my confidence for the future·

Milo Challenges You:
Let us try a little exercise now! Write down as many things you can think of that you have achieved.

It could be something like passing a test, improving in a subject/task or even a colleague/teacher offering you praise. Perhaps it's something you received a certificate for or an event you completed. Have you helped someone or is there something that you find quite easy to do every time you do it?

Fun Facts – Quality not quantity
As you can see, winning isn't everything. In fact, all of the following were runners up in *X-Factor* and went on to do OK for themselves in music. Rebecca Ferguson came second in 2010, Olly Murs was second in 2009 and One Direction were amazingly third in 2010. Never heard of them? Look them up then!

P is for Practice – Practice Makes Progress

"The more I practise, the luckier I get." – Gary Player (professional golfer) *

The weekend had arrived as soon as the Friday school bell sounded for the final time of the week. Yesterday's exam was a distant memory as a wave of students headed for the school exit. Chatter, laughter and excitement could be heard as the crowds rushed passed Mrs Lombardi and Mr Switchblade, who were both on duty.

Milo wandered towards them with Rico, Fidelma and others. Rico was carrying his guitar; the wannabe rock star one day, he had shrugged off the need for serious study. As far as he was concerned, if he could read music then that was all he needed to know.

Mr Switchblade called out, "Hey Milo, thirty press ups, yes thirty," and raised his thumbs up to notify them of his progress. "Have a great weekend and remember, practice makes progress."

He raised his thumb again and then mimicked a book-reading action, this must be the title of the next chapter.

"Is Switch still going on about that press-up thing?" Rico asked.

"Yep, he's doing great and he's not a bad guy either. Not as scary as people think!"

"Anyway, he's wrong, everyone knows practice makes PERFECT!"

Milo ignored the last statement as he thought that Switch may have a point with something and he couldn't be bothered to argue with Rico on that subject. It was the weekend and a group of them had formed as they walked out of the gate, there were more important topics to cover. It's the weekend!

Five of them were off to Big Dan's Bowling Alley that evening for a bit of a friendly bowling competition. Rico and Milo had tickets to watch their local football team on Saturday afternoon and they were meeting another friend Noah there. Rico had his guitar lesson and Milo had been given an important piece of English coursework so he had planned in some time to get that started plus there was time to read his next Future Toolbox chapter as he'd been skipping this at weekends.

As Rico still wasn't really sold on all this learning and personal development, he added a bit of peer pressure to Milo in an attempt to get him to pop over to his house, saying he could play some new songs he had learned instead. The two lads loved the same type of music so it was an extremely tempting offer but Milo decided to be good and stick to his original plan.

Rico was dedicated to his guitar and would practise for hours on end and Milo was full of respect for his dedication. In fact, he was a little jealous that he could master some great tunes that Milo wished he could play himself.

Practice makes...
Most people want to finish that statement by saying the word **perfect**. Is it possible to be perfect all of the time? The answer is no. First, we must remove the need for perfection. Remember in **Y is for Your Life**, the natural wonders of the world are not airbrushed and **John Legend** sang about **"All your perfect imperfections!"** In fact, the only person who is Practically Perfect in Every Way is Mary Poppins.

Practice makes progress.
It is fair to say that the more you **practise** something, the better you will become. **Practice**, repetitions, multiple rehearsals – whatever you want to call it – are the key to **progress** which leads to success.

- Actors rehearse and repeat their lines over and over again until the final scene is cut.
- Musicians practise playing musical instruments or singing lyrics before the performance is given.
- Sportspeople train and train and train over and over again to maximise their performance in events.
- What about successful workers, professionals and business owners? They train and develop themselves in their specialised fields to become masters in their trades.
- Academic students who study and revise more achieve better quality results.
- Pilots clock up flying hours. A pilot is never judged how long they have been a pilot, they are asked how many flying hours they have.

Warning.
Sadly, there are no shortcuts to achieve mastery but we all look for the easy button. It doesn't exist.

Can you remember the words to your favourite song? How about the scenes in your number one film of all time? Bet you've heard that song or seen that film numerous times, haven't you? Of course, you can… and why is that? Well you have probably heard that song over and over again or watched that film a few times.

How about if someone asked you to describe your journey from home to school/work/a friend's/family member's home? You would be able to describe the route if you have made this journey many times before.

Again, the key to you successfully completing any of the tasks above is multiple repetitions.

It was teatime and Milo was reading whilst eating before heading to Big Dan's Bowling Alley. The idea of practice was evident with everyone around him; his sister would be constantly rehearsing drama lines and dance moves; Mum was practicing some lines for her business presentation next week; Dad's running programme; his own revision plan. Rico and his guitar of course.

Beep, beep! The car horn sounded outside! Milo crammed the last mouthful of food in his mouth, put the plate in the dishwasher and shouted a quick goodbye as he ran out of the door. There sat Rico and his dad in their silver car, ready to give him a lift.

Milo hopped in the back and clicked his seatbelt into place. Before being able to say hello, Rico pointed at the car radio and raised his hand for silence. The song broke into a guitar riff and Rico mimicked playing it himself as he sat in the front seat. The band U2 was on near full volume as the car pulled away.

Rico's dad allowed the song to finish, as he was a big fan of the band, before lowering the volume slightly.

The radio continued to engage the occupants of the car, as the show was about the band and an interview with the lead singer, Bono. The presenter closed the chatter by acknowledging that Bono was off to rehearse in the studio. For a band that was established in 1976.

"So, Bono, after all these years, you still need to practise?"

"Yep, indeed. We still need to build the foundations for our next performance or recording. That's, what has made us so successful." The show ended and the news headlines began so Rico hit the off button and Milo was first to speak,

"Practice makes progress!"

"Ooh, I like that," Rico's dad replied with approval. "The band U2 still going strong after over forty years. In fact, I saw them long before you were both born."

"Yes, their key to mastery was consistent practice and multiple rehearsals. The best never stop improving themselves; another piece of real evidence from a programme I'm following at school called the Future Toolbox," Milo smartly pointed out.

The conversation about music continued until they arrived at Big Dan's Bowling Alley and the group of five met up. Big Dan showed them to their lane and the competition began. Noah scored the highest over the two games narrowly beating Rico with Molly third, Milo fourth and Fidelma last.

"Be the best you can be. I gave it my best shot" Fidelma said, quoting from Q is for Quality and accepting that her bowling skills needed a lot more practice.

The following day after the football match, Milo got home and sat on the sofa before eating his tea. He picked up his book and thought about the points of practice he had seen in the past couple of days.

The more you practise, the more effort you put in and the harder you try, the more luck will come your way.

Sometimes we have to fail to hit our target a few times in order to get a bit of luck and sometimes we have to keep persisting but sometimes it will happen.

Practise Getting Lucky.
Do you ever feel that some people have all the luck, right?

They seem to have great talent and be brilliant at whatever they do; singing, dancing, sport, have loads of money, brilliant communication skills, the air of confidence, they look great in whatever they wear... the list is endless. What's more, they appear to achieve this effortlessly with very few knock backs.

There is a phrase that goes along the lines, "If you fall in poo, then you always come out smelling of roses!"
Isn't that just soooo unfair?

Truth is, it's not! These guys create the luck; remember the quote from golfer Arnold Palmer at the start of this chapter? **The more you practise, the luckier you get**. Momentum then kicks in and it seems more natural.

Milo sat back in his chair, put his hands behind his head and thought about the examples from his weekend:
1. **Firstly the radio interview – a band of forty years still practising to remain masters of their trade.**
2. **At the bowling alley, Fidelma was there in the group of school mates. She had never bowled before in her life but on her first effort, she hit all ten pins down and got a strike. Brilliant... how lucky. Some might say, beginner's luck!**

However, how many pins did she hit with her next shot? ... and the next... and the next? Well it wasn't ten! In fact, she didn't get another strike all night and finished last in the scoring. Although she enjoyed the evening and had lots of fun, she realised she certainly wasn't a master at bowling – not yet, anyway!

3. At the football match on Saturday afternoon, Milo, Rico and Noah's team were level at 1-1. In the last minute, a player took a shot at goal. He stubbed his toe into the ground and stumbled forward, losing control of the ball. Although he made a poor connection on the ball, it still trickled past the goalkeeper and into the goal. The lad cheered the winning goal but in truth – it was lucky. Again, here was an example of a professional who had put in hours of practice... the more practice he puts in, the luckier he gets at times.

There are various types of luck in the world:
Random good luck is like a winning lottery ticket. Fidelma experienced this with her first strike, as she had no control over the outcome.
Opportunity luck is what the footballer experienced; he had taken many shots in his career and created opportunity after opportunity until it came good. Gary Player took many golf shots in his career which helped him win nine major championships in the 1960s and 1970s.

There are also some opposites to the above:
Random bad luck would be something you also have no control over but without such good consequences – getting struck by lightning, for example.
Detrimental luck is created by continuous poor choices. For example, a business owner who makes continuous poor choices over the finances and eventually the company goes bust.

Laying Foundations.
When I used to work full time at an office in the town centre, I would walk to work past a big building site and noticed the workforce appeared to make very little **progress** in the first few months? The earth was constantly being flattened and holes were dug and filled in but there was no sign of any building, just bits of metal and concrete poking out of the ground. Suddenly, in the space of a few weeks, a huge office block rises from the ground and towers over the street below. It seemed to take more time to lay the foundations and less time to build the structure and completely furnish the offices for habitation.

The key to a safe building is a strong foundation.
Sometimes we have to apply that principle to our lives. Do the preparation in order to perfect the action and get the results.

Ever cooked a meal that has taken longer to prepare and cook than it did to eat?

So we must always prepare in order to achieve our successes and keep repeating those **practices** in order to master your destiny. Find out what is needed to succeed and then **practise** it.

Milo's Toolbox:
Sometimes you will get lucky immediately but the real success comes from consistent practice.
The more I keep practising, the luckier I will get.
Remember, don't strive for perfection, aim to be your best.

Milo Challenges You:
Lay your foundations for a solid structure for success.

What could you put a bit more **practice** in to develop yourself?

Perhaps it is a new challenge or maybe something you are already aiming to become a master of?

Evaluate your plan and get to work on your multiple rehearsals.

Fun Facts – Practice makes weirdness

Practice makes **progress** and sometimes you ask yourself if it was all worth it in the end. Well these guys are probably still asking that question.

Paul Prado and catcher Sophia Rojas set a world record for the farthest marshmallow to be blown out of a nostril and into the mouth of a catcher. Erghhh, Sophia was the catcher standing 5.46 metres (17 ft 11 in) away in 2012. Lots of **practice** and lots of snotty marshmallows.

Hours spent clipping clothes pegs to his face helped Italian Silvio Sabba achieve his dream world record of fifty-one pegs in one minute in 2012.

Li Longlong must have turned the world upside down when he set his record for the most consecutive stairs climbed on his head. The total of thirty-six and was achieved in China in 2015.

All that **practice** must have been stressful so this could be a little simpler! Slovakia's Pavol Ďurdik holds the record for the most socks put on one foot in one minute which was fifty-two in 2017. We're not sure what these people have gone onto achieve since but at least they will always have a story to tell their grandkids.

* There was some debate about whether it was Arnold Palmer or fellow golfer Gary Player actually said this quote first but whoever it was, it's certainly true of practice making progress.

O is for Open Your Mind –
Look Through the Door Before You Slam It Shut

"If someone offers you an amazing opportunity and you're not sure you can do it, say yes – then learn how to do it later."– Richard Branson (business entrepreneur)

Sunday morning and no alarm clock sounded but Milo woke up at a reasonable time. He used to sometimes sleep until midday but was pleased to see the time was just gone 9 a.m.

"This sleep pattern is really working," he thought to himself. His mind began to wander, thinking over the past few weeks since he discovered the Future Toolbox. The family had noticed a change in him, instead of keeping himself to himself, he was chattier when at home. The relationship with Thea was still improving as they were laughing more and enjoying each other's company instead of both always trying to be right and prove their egos were bigger than each other. Somehow, he had new energy levels that didn't exist before, perhaps due to changes in sleep patterns and eating a little more healthily. At school, teachers seemed to be more approachable and helpful. The truth is, they were always helpful but his personal development made him realise that they were really decent people who wanted to help him succeed. He even found it easy to have great conversations with Mr Switchblade who had seemed the scariest and most unapproachable person in the world before. Finally, simple planning and organisation seemed a little easier and Milo realised that they were his own responsibility now (or at least he had the ability to respond). The person who was most surprised and affected by all of these small changes was Milo himself.

After listening to a bit of music, Milo got to his feet, switched off the volume and picked up his weekly planner. The coursework needed doing. Mum had some people visiting later for the business presentation and he'd volunteered to help set up the living room and make refreshments. There was an educational television documentary on later too; it would be useful to watch but not essential if time ran out. Catch-up TV is a saviour as a backup plan. There were around forty-five minutes until everyone came home so he decided to read a little.

Open or closed mind?
Have you ever said no to something without giving any thought to what you have actually said no to? Read that question again and then answer again!

We all do this from time to time – criticise an idea before seeing the big picture or offer an objection before seeking a way forward. Perhaps seeing the negative before the positive or quitting before we've even begun trying. Some people are more negative and closed-minded than others and they become stuck in their ways.

This is all down to mindsets at the time and our result will depend on how **open** or closed minded we are. **Be open, be brave, be adventurous.**

Sometimes it is in the moments of decision that your destiny is shaped.

If an opportunity is presented and it seems like the right choice, now is the time to seize the moment. Unfortunately, too many people close their mind quickly and effectively miss out. They slam the door shut, usually with an excuse such as:

- "Oooh it's too hard, I couldn't do that!"
- "I haven't got the time, I'm far too busy!"
- "I haven't got the skills or confidence!"
- "So and so tried that and it didn't work for them so it won't work for me!"

Does this sound mightily familiar to the *U Can Do It – Silence the "I Can't"* chapter?

Now of course, not every opportunity is going to suit everyone and some people will actually have genuine limitations. Perhaps the timing isn't right now but if you are going to say no, make it a no for now. Leave the door slightly ajar and then you can return in the future.

Dad arrived home from a run and Thea wandered down from her room at the same time so Milo's reading was interrupted. He knew his mum would be keen to get the house in order before everyone arrived so he paused for a moment and scribbled down a quick note in his journal. "Be open minded; look for the "I can" and then headed to join the hustle and bustle.

An hour later, the family had eaten and the house was set up for the guests arriving. Thea was back upstairs doing her homework, Dad was manning the teacups ready for the influx of kettle boiling

and Milo was hovering around by the front door on standby as the meet-and-greet man.

First to arrive was Michael the Mentor who was there to support Mum in her first steps; having a like-minded person to guide you in the early days is a valuable asset to success. The excitement was building as Mum and Michael the Mentor were setting up the television to show a short video to explain the business. The doorbell sounded and guests began arriving one by one. Milo was taking coats and showing them through to the living room but most descended to the kitchen to see Dad in full flow making the teas and coffees. Chatter and laughter sounded throughout the house and Mum was flitting between conversations, slowly trying to usher everyone to their seats. She was a little outside his comfort zone but nervously excited.

After some introductions and general chit-chat, it was time for the presentation to begin. Mum asked Milo if he would like to stay in the room and be part of the rest of the event.

"Hmm, be open minded," he muttered to himself. "Yes, I will stay, Mum, thank you."

His mind raced. The guests, all adults, some he knew and some he didn't. They would all see something new and Milo felt he wanted to stay and find out what he could learn. Pulling up a foot stool, he perched himself in the corner of the room next to Wall Street Waz and the presentation began.

Owning the room, Michael was confident and explained the benefits of the home-based business opportunity that Milo's mum had recently begun. The theme of the event was to simply share information about the benefits of becoming involved as a customer or business partner but nobody would be expected to make a solid decision there and then. Phrases such as "open minded" and "motivated" were used by Michael in the presentation.

After a short fifteen minutes, the presentation drew to a close and a few questions were asked. Milo sat back and observed how Michael listened and answered them confidently. Although Milo didn't understand some of the information, it all sounded really positive and exciting.

Following the questions, the group broke into general chatter and Milo joined his dad in the kitchen, carrying a few empty cups to help out. A couple who were long-term family friends were chatting to Dad and sharing their opinions on the presentation and they were quite critical.

"Ah yes, it was good but it won't be for us. You know we have been customers of xyz and don't like change. As for the opportunity, well we're not really good at stuff like that and we don't have the time anyway."

"Closed-minded, lack of self-belief, barriers and excuses," Milo thought to himself as he smiled at his dad and headed back towards the living room. This boy is learning fast!

Mum and Michael were engrossed in a conversation with a lady called Roxanne who had been a good friend of Mum's for years and they were talking at a fast and excited pace. They turned to include Milo in the conversation and Roxanne commented on how polite he always is. She was a happy, smiley person and he always loved chatting to her when she popped round.

Putting her hand on his shoulder, Roxanne said to Milo, "Isn't your mum wonderful? You should be proud of her, starting this venture for her family." Her smile grew bigger as she turned to his mum and continued, "Well you know me, I respect everything you do and I would love to support you. Let's meet up for a coffee in the week and we can chat. I'm open minded to find out a bit more."

Her body language was relaxed, her arms were open but most importantly, Milo noticed, so was her mind!

The event drew to a close and the guests dispersed one by one until only Michael was left. He was an inspirational person who had gained the respect of everyone in attendance that evening. His confidence, posture and belief had remained consistently high throughout. Although Milo had only met him once briefly, he felt comfortable in his presence. He had been referred to as an entrepreneur and you could tell why he was successful. The laws of attraction recommend you to hang around successful people so Milo knew he had made a good choice to be part of the evening. Although there were still a lot of things he didn't understand about this business, the complicated sounding parts and how an entrepreneur fully functioned, he remained open minded to keep learning.

After Michael left, the family chatted and Milo made it clear that he wanted to be involved in helping at more of these types of events. His mum and dad were delighted.

Later that evening, Milo sat in bed and finished the chapter in his Future Toolbox **book**.

Open your mind to learning.
Study is the key to enhancing your mind but here is a bold statement.

"School is borrrrrrrrringgggggg!"

Aha, time to change the way you think and open your mind. Some of us are still there as students or teachers and some of us left many years ago. The authorities make it the law for us to all attend school for our own good. It is a place to go to learn skills for the future but not everything will suit everyone of course.

Now everyone should go to school (boring or not) – we should go to learn the basics and learn social skills. There are some amazing teachers out there in some amazing schools too.

The curriculum is the curriculum but it has been mentioned earlier in this book that you should learn as much as you can and throw away what you don't need, later. This is as open-minded as anyone can be of any age. A teen can do this at school and an adult can do this at work. We can all pick up a book, watch an educational programme or listen to an inspirational person on audio or even face to face.

Unfortunately, some people leave compulsory education and decide to quit learning. Why not look at trying new worthwhile things to enhance your mind? New experiences, new foods, new places with new people, new challenges – some that may scare you perhaps, new studies, new learning, travel.

A study of open-minded students.
Here is a great example of a study carried out by the **Future Toolbox** coaches.

In further education, A-Level students are encouraged to become independent learners; this means going to as many different sources as they can and seeking different opinions, arguments and angles on a topic. Imagine Student A goes online and types a subject into a search engine. They select three or four websites and write a report on the findings before handing in a five-page essay to their tutor.

The tutor marks their work (probably alongside the twenty or so other pieces) and they are pretty uninspired by the many similar answers by classmates who have followed a similar internet research pattern.

However, Student B takes their project and decides to spend an hour or so in the museum, wandering around at their own pace, taking notes and, if allowed, a few pictures on their smartphone. They then head to a pre-arranged appointment with a local expert at a local coffee shop and on the way, they slip into the library, pick a book of the shelf and make a couple of notes from it before heading to meet the expert. The expert spends fifteen minutes chatting with them and the student buys them a coffee to say thank you. That evening, the student watches a TV documentary that lasts for thirty minutes and gives some more information on the topic. The five-page report is produced and handed in to the tutor.

Question – who is the going to get the best marks? Student A or Student B?

Every time the **Future Toolbox** team poses this scenario to a tutor in further education, they always go for Student B of course.

Marks aside though, who is going to be most inspired? Student A or Student B?

Student B is the most affected by the whole experience.

More importantly, Student B gets the biggest benefit. Yes, the tutor is going to be inspired and impressed to give better marks on the work but did Student B do it to make the tutor's career more fulfilling? Ultimately, they are going to be the most fulfilled by their **open-minded** approach to learning as they have expanded their mind with a wealth of mindful information.

Be more like Student B.
Go above and beyond sometimes and feed your brain with awesome knowledge. You never know when you'll find the answer.

A friend of ours who is a mature student noticed in lectures, many of the students who were there straight from school would ask if the information the lecturer was giving would be in the final exams. If the lecturer said it wouldn't, over 75% of them chose not to write it down. Why would you pay tens of thousands of pounds to study a degree and not bother learning absolutely everything? We need to feed our minds with as much as we possibly can. Be more like Student B.

Why do the minimum when you can go the extra mile? Feed your mind with personal development.
So, what could you learn from? You choose:
- Completing a level on a computer game OR completing an inspirational book.
- Reading a story about which celeb has been divorced, checked into rehab or been caught doing something they allegedly

shouldn't have been doing OR reading a story about an inspirational person, achieving inspirational things.

- Instant messaging your friends every minute to find out what they have been doing since you last instant messaged them a minute ago OR spending time having a conversation with your family, sharing the art of conversation.
- Watching a far-fetched television programme based around scandal, drugs, sex scenes, killing or suchlike OR watching a documentary about something factual like a life story, true story, nature, the world or a quiz programme loaded with knowledge and answers.
- A viral video about a person falling over, a guy performing a silly trick or a something that has over 2.4m views and it really isn't that funny OR an online interview with a world leader, entrepreneur or champion in an area that interests you, a how-to video on how to learn something amazing or a video on how to make studying fun.

Prejudgement.

To finish this chapter, let's add one more tool into our **Future Toolbox** to help ourselves become better people. Since building our businesses, one top tip we picked up from successful leaders is to never **prejudge** someone. You never know who they are until you know them. To judge something before you know it can make you form an incorrect opinion and close your mind. This can sometimes block something that could end up being invaluable and this doesn't just apply to people. Some people will tell you they don't like something before they have tried it.

Learn not to **prejudge** people on their: background, race, size, sex, age, area, background, accent, appearance.

Use your judgement to follow instinct and trust judgement of experts and not so-called experts who are misinformed people.

Milo's Toolbox:

Be open minded and never close a door before taking a peek into the room· It may lead to an opportunity·

Look for opportunities and study successful people·

Understand how to become an entrepreneur·

Milo Challenges You:

Think of times where you have dismissed something recently without giving it much thought. Perhaps you made an excuse or didn't really focus on what was presented to you. Now see if there is a way you can reopen the door to the opportunity. Perhaps if a person offered you something and you said no, you could go back and ask them if the opportunity still exists.

Try something new. Maybe a food you haven't tasted before, a type of music that someone has recommended but you haven't heard, a place you haven't visited, a book you haven't read, something you have yet to learn.

Fun Facts – Open your mind and try this

We have suggested that you be **open-minded** but we may draw the line at trying these foods from around the world.

You could have Tuna Eyeballs in Japan or Century Egg in China – it's actually just a rotten egg, it's not 100 years old. Maybe eat Jing Leed, which are grasshoppers in Thailand or Wasp Crackers in Japan Yep, it's a biscuit filled with wasps, instead of chocolate chip in cookies, replace the choccy chips with wasps. Don't fancy this for sure.

Go to Cambodia and have fried spider or in France you can sample escargots à la bourguignonne which are basically snails. In Africa there are stink bugs on the menu and in Sardinia, Italy it's maggot cheese. Even right here in the UK we have pickled eggs and jellied eels from your local chip shop that are an acquired taste.

However, if you like living on the edge, let's go back to Japan one more time and try fugu a blowfish which is deadly if not prepared properly. You can try it if you want, we're not!

N is for No Time Like the Present –
It's Now or Never

"Education is the passport for the future, for tomorrow belongs to those who prepare for it today!" – Malcolm X (human rights activist)

Procrastination! Ever put something off because you are too busy doing other stuff to avoid doing the stuff you should be doing? Of course you have, everyone's guilty of procrastinating. In fact, some people don't even get around to procrastinating because they procrastinate too much. That may sound like a poor joke but, truth is, it's in our nature to find an excuse to put off doing a task that we don't like doing. Other factors can come into play such as lacking self-belief, distractions or plain and simply being too lazy.

As he read these words from the book, Milo scratched his head and raised his eyebrows. The week had been really busy so far. Monday, the day after his mum's business launch, it was back to school for the start of another week. He was part of a group that had volunteered to clear out a classroom which took a few days. In the evenings he had met up with some friends and had a family get together too. The cross-country team had also added an extra session on Tuesday to prepare for the race which was just over a week away.

Suddenly Thursday evening had arrived and he sat in his room after school. A pile of homework sat on his desk next to a pile of revision and his Future Toolbox book and journal were on the chair beside the desk. He knew the work needed doing but he just couldn't be bothered and his hand was hovering above the "on" button of the TV remote. Perhaps a quick episode of Lily the Looter's Virtual Crime World wouldn't hurt.

Four hours later, his mum wandered into the room to check he was still alive but she was soon shooed away because a key moment of the programme was happening.

Suddenly it was 10 o'clock and Milo found his eyes hurting under the strain of the television box set watch-a-thon. There was one episode left. Have you ever tried leaving a cliff-hanger until the following day? It was plain and simple, it needed watching. He rubbed his eyes, considered leaving it until the following day and then did was most people would do... yep, he watched it.

The storyline finished with a real twist right at the end. Milo pulled himself upright from the pillow as the closing credits rolled up the TV screen. Still lost in the moment of the show, his eyes scanned around his room in an attempt to snap out of television mode and into the real world. Suddenly, that fear of panic jumped into the pit of his stomach as he saw it right there on top of the pile – the coursework he had been given last Friday.

Oh nooooo! Milo leapt up and dashed over to his desk, knocking a pot of pens onto the floor. Staring him in the face on his weekly planner were the words "Coursework – hand in Friday". It was in the URGENT IMPORTANT box! Oh nooooo, panic started to set in.

He had had good intentions of doing the work since the weekend but kept putting it off because he found it a little boring and other things had started to take priority.

After a couple of stressful hours battling his body clock, Milo finally put down his pen and switched off the light around 1:30 a.m. He knew the quality of his work wasn't great but it would have to do now.

The following day was tough and lacked that usual "Friday feeling". Milo was tired and grouchy and he was struggling to focus. As the bell sounded, everyone made their way to the exits but English teacher, Patrick Paragraph, stepped into Milo's path and informed him that his English project wasn't up to standard. He had missed a whole section out.

"Great," he thought to himself as he took the work from Mr Paragraph's hand, "more homework to fit into this weekend." He knew he had rushed his way through the project so it was hardly surprising but to add to the misery, Mrs Lombardi stopped him at the school gates and engaged in conversation about the Future Toolbox and what he had learned that week. He hadn't been reading the book but he soon gathered that the topic on procrastination was the main focus. Ironically, he had been a victim of this all week; no homework and no journal, just television.

Rather than make an excuse or make up a story, he decided to think of his ability to respond and committed to a little extra work over the weekend.

So here we are on Saturday morning, after a week of neglect. Milo began reading.

Danger.

When procrastinating, people either let a distraction or an excuse get in the way of their success, but the danger is putting the task off so many times that the goal slips out of reach.

For example, many people say, "I will do it tomorrow" or pick a life event and set a loose timescale based on the date for achieving. They put it back again, again and again until they regret not seizing the opportunity.

OK, the title of this chapter includes the statement, "It's now or never". Sometimes you get one shot and one shot only but there are ways of reopening a door and getting a second chance.

Many adults have common regrets as their state education disappears into their life's memory. Below are common themes when talking to people over the age of thirty when looking back on their teenage years:

- Not spending time with friends, parents and family and also not appreciating them more.
- Being lazy with my body, eating the wrong things and not exercising more.
- Spending too much time worrying what others thought of me – wearing too much make up/aftershave/perfume/choosing clothes to impress others.
- Not volunteering more and doing things to lift the spirits of others.
- Giving up too easily on my school/education and not embracing my learning.
- Getting involved with the wrong crowd or getting into trouble.

These are only a small handful of examples but there is one common theme; they all include procrastination in one form or another. Whatever age you are, ask yourself, do any of the above statements sound familiar to me now? Then ask yourself, is it too late to make changes?

- Could you get in touch with those you may have lost touch with?
- What changes could you make to your diet or what exercise plan could you begin?

- Those people you spent many years trying to impress, are they still impressed? Do they really care? Do you even know them now? Do you really care? Who is important to you now?
- What could you volunteer to do?
- What new things could you learn?

Below are the top regrets of the elderly in the final years of their lives:
- I wish I had travelled the world more.
- I wish I had been more adventurous.
- I wish I had been smarter with money and saved more.
- I wish I hadn't spent so much time working on my career and spent more time with family, friends and loved ones.

The final regret on the above list involves time; it is certainly something that will pass. As mentioned in *T is for Time*, it is not something we can bank and carry over to another day, week, month or year. Sometimes the moment has to be seized; the opportunity grabbed with both hands, taking the leap of faith. As Richard Branson said (in **O is for Open Your Mind**), "'If someone offers you an amazing opportunity and you're not sure you can do it, say yes – then learn how to do it later!"

Milo sighed but then smiled to himself as the moment of irony hit home. All week he had procrastinated and let distractions take over before leaving everything until the last minute. This resulted in creating panic and stress and extra work had to be done at the weekend at the sacrifice of some fun activities.

By the evening, the English project was complete. He chatted to Fidelma about her progress and she admitted that she too was guilty of a disastrous week from time to time. Here was a top student going off track; this felt reassuring that it wasn't just him.

His mum proofread his work and was impressed. Milo was honest and told her that things hadn't gone to plan. Yep, she was guilty too, only that week she was supposed to follow up some business prospects but had put it off and still not called them. "In fact, I'll ring them in a moment," she declared.

His Saturday had suffered and he was tired so it was definitely time for bed. Time to reset the body-clock and get some rest.

Milo's Toolbox:
Make a plan and stick to it where possible·
Make a start on tasks early rather than leaving them until the last minute·
We all procrastinate from time to time but don't beat myself up if I do· Be honest with myself and re-plan if this happens·

Milo Challenges You:
Here is Milo's challenge – pick a task and make a plan well in advance and start work sooner rather than later.

For example, if it is a task that is due in ten days' time, make the plan on day one and draw out a simple timeline of steps to achieving it on time.

Make sure you have all the tools required.

Display the plan in prominent places and view it regularly to stay on track.

If the task is something that you are not going to enjoy, perhaps suitably reward yourself upon completion.

Fun Facts – Procrast… erm I'll get round to finishing the word later
The world is full of procrastinators! Leonardo De Vinci had a very short attention span and used to pay musicians to play for him to keep him focussed whilst painting. It didn't always work though because most of

his paintings are incomplete. It even took him over fifteen years to complete the Mona Lisa. Then there was Victor Hugo, writer of the famous play, *Les Miserables*. Instead of focussing on writing, he preferred going to parties. One day, he decided to knuckle down and got his servants to lock away his party clothes so he could finish the play. Hmm, now who can we ask to turn the mobile phone off?

M is for Meditation – Time to Relax

"Half an hour's meditation each day is essential, except when you are busy. Then a full hour is needed." – Saint Francis de Sales (Patron Saint of the Deaf, Journalists and Writers)

Ever had the moment of panic when you feel that something is about to go horribly wrong and yet everything actually ends up going completely to plan? You probably spent hours, days or even weeks worrying and it was totally unnecessary. In fact, sometimes the result was even better than you expected, wasn't it?

Stress and anxiety are probably higher in all age groups than it has ever been. Even children as young as primary school age are reported to be suffering. In truth, much of this pain is actually needless.

Did you know?
Of over 90% of things that people worry about, the worry is **completely unnecessary**; a waste of time and energy.

So how do we reduce stress?
M is for meditation gives the impression that you are going to sit in a yoga position and start chanting Ohm. That is not for everyone but feel free to try it. It is perhaps a good idea to start simple first though.

The thought of sitting legs crossed and chanting made Milo chuckle to himself. He sat in his favourite chair, reading his next Future Toolbox **lesson. It was quiet, as Dad was out running, Mum had a business appointment and Thea was upstairs watching TV in her room. He was still recovering from the stress after the procrastination over the English project, of course. It is easy now to see what factors had contributed to the rising stress levels but at the time, it isn't always that obvious. Milo sometimes felt quite anxious about being a failure, especially at study and more so, sport. He read on...**

The tell-tale signs.
The first step to **stress management** is to recognise what stress actually is. Here is a simple analogy:

Fight or flight.
When an animal is attacked in the wild, it will react by fighting its attacker and scaring it off or even killing it or it will run away and hide. It will remain in its hiding place until it is safe to come out. The other option is to freeze and pray for the best but this doesn't normally end well.

We can liken **fight or flight** to us as human beings and the way we react to stress.

Fight mode.
We are going to talk about **instant stress** for the moment. Fight mode can kick in when you feel **threatened**. Imagine you have been given some really harsh criticism and it has really hurt you.

132

The lion has attacked you!
The hormone **adrenaline** has been released and you have gone into **fight mode**, ready to hit back at the lion. You snarl and show your teeth before lashing out in defence.

The lion continues to attack you. In this instance, you have been criticised and you defended yourself. The person who criticised you (the lion) isn't happy either and the situation could potentially end in a full-blown row. The lion could back off or be killed but you could end up being the victim too. In real life, we know the result of a row is always a difficult and awkward situation.

Flight mode.
Let's take the exact same situation but imagine you reacted in the opposite manner. You receive the criticism and adrenaline kicks in making you feel upset but this time you go into **flight mode**.

You have been attacked by the lion!
The adrenaline makes you run! You run and run getting faster and faster and jump into some bushes. Peering through the leaves, you see the coast is clear and the lion cannot be seen. What happens next is the key:

Anxiety kicks in.
The lion may have turned in the opposite direction but you are faced with some scary choices. Will it be back? Should you stay in your hiding place or step out into the open? Are there any other lions prowling around? The problem may have gone for now but you are licking your wounds.

In this instance, when you received the criticism, your reaction was minimal. You took it on board and walked away, almost accepting it without perhaps asking for explanations or seeking solutions.

When away from the confrontation, you are still displaying the tell-tale signs of stress including:
- Anger – why did the lion attack me? Is this personal?

133

- Stomach churning – the adrenaline is whizzing around like a washing machine. Perhaps I am a failure, I should just give in and let the lion eat me.
- Feeling of apprehension – what should I do if the lion returns and attacks again?
- Wanting to react – perhaps I should go and seek out this lion and when he's not looking – bam! Yeah, that'll teach him for daring to criticise me.

This is where anxiety kicks in. There's a belief that stress and anxiety are the same but stress is a response to a threat in a situation and anxiety can be a reaction to the stress.

Imagine you are waiting for some news from someone, say the answer for a job interview or the result of a test. Perhaps you have asked someone a favour or maybe on a date. Then a letter arrives, an email in your inbox or a text message or phone call and you know it is from the person who is making the decision and you are about to find the answer.

Some people immediately fear the worst and go into flight mode and anxiety kicks in. They worry that the news will be bad before they know what the result or outcome is. This is where the needless stress happens because the decision has been made and nothing is going to change it whether it is positive or negative.

Suddenly, there was a loud bang from upstairs as his sister slammed the bedroom door shut before stomping loudly down the stairs. She was chatting loudly on her mobile phone whilst giggling with her friend Melissa who could be heard on loudspeaker.

The peace and quiet had been shattered and Milo was now instantly irritated. He couldn't understand why the phone had to be on loudspeaker and thought that a conversation between two people didn't need to be shared with everyone in earshot.

He shot her a look but she responded by sticking her tongue out before wandering into the kitchen, slamming the door behind her.

It was now fight or flight time – does he:
1. Chase into the kitchen and give her a piece of his mind? She needs to be considerate to him and should be told.
2. Ignore the noise and hope that she quietens down a bit?
3. Wander into the kitchen, smile and ask her nicely if she would mind being a little quieter?

He chose option 2 and hoped that his sister would quieten down and the problem would go away, leaving him to go back to reading his book.

Unfortunately, the noise continued and appeared to get even louder, which disrupted his reading even more. Enough was enough; he jumped from his seat and stormed towards the kitchen door. Heart racing, hands sweating, adrenaline pumping, he hovered his hand above the door handle but suddenly stopped. The next passage of the book had been a bit of a blur but it had stayed in his subconscious mind.

Hit the pause button.
Imagine that the stressful situation in front of you is a movie and you are the lead character. Before the adrenaline takes over you, hit the **pause button** and take a quick look at the freeze-frame of the screen in front of you. Now assess the situation and ask yourself:
- How important is this situation to the rest of my life? Will it last forever or will it pass and things change?
- Remind yourself that everything in life will pass and form a plan to remove the stress. Work out what you can or can't control. What you can do to practically change things or if you have to accept the situation and work with it.

If you can't manage your plan, then call upon someone who can help and support you... and then smile. **Remain focussed on the solution and not the problem.**

These steps are helpful for removing a minor crisis and immediate stress but need modifying for major stress and serious incidents. Practise slowing down your thinking and use your pause button to give yourself a moment to react – perhaps the major crisis can be avoided.

His hand was still hovering above the door handle; Milo had hit the pause button. He was assessing the situation; there he was standing outside the kitchen and Thea was inside, completely unaware of how irritating she was being. The chatter on the phone, clattering of plates and slamming of cupboard doors was unacceptable.

The draft assessment.
You can't control some circumstances and you certainly can't change some people. It is a little bit like the weather; sometimes it will rain and sometimes it will be too hot. Could you run outside and shout at the sky to change the climate to suit you? Of course not, so why do we try and control the things we are unable to control?

Sometimes people will be noisy or have habits and traits that you don't like. Maybe they don't realise that they irritate you or perhaps you have been the lion and criticised them in the wrong way in the past and they are in flight mode. Aha, that makes sense, doesn't it?

What was Thea doing? Perhaps the conversation is important. How is her mood? Will the situation last long-term? Will it affect me in thirty minutes, never mind for the rest of my life? Is there a solution or compromise?

Milo took a deep breath in, let it out and opened the kitchen door slowly… and then smiled.

"Hey Sis, what's up?"

"Hey Milo," came the friendly response from his sister as she stirred some ingredients into a mixing bowl. "I'm making a meal for Mum and Dad and Melissa is helping me on the phone. She is an expert on making incredibly tasty, healthy food and I needed her advice."

"Wow that's amazing," replied Milo, licking his lips. "I don't suppose you could turn the speaker down on your phone a little so I can concentrate on my reading?"

"Sure thing bro, Melissa says hi too."

Tame the lion.
On this occasion, the lion had been tamed. Thea's noise was the stressor and he could have fought back. On this occasion he decided to reason with the issue and saved a lot of stress.

Let us look at the alternative option; Milo opens the door and storms in shouting, "I'm trying to read, (swear word) keep it down!"

His sister reacts by slamming down the mixing bowl and shouting, "I'm making a meal for Mum and Dad and it would be nice if you would do something for them for once. You think you're so perfect because you're studying (insert your own words to finish sentence)."

The situation escalates into a full-blown row. She storms off upstairs in a huff, throwing down the mixing bowl whilst moaning to her friend Melissa about how bad her brother is. Milo tried to go back to read but can't concentrate because he is angry and the kitchen is now in a mess of half-made meal. When Mum and Dad arrive home, they are annoyed at the state of the house so both siblings get into trouble.

The pause button definitely worked and Milo chose the better option by diffusing his stress before it had a chance to get out of control. You could even say that he didn't agitate the lion in the first place.

It's not that straightforward.
There are thousands of books on **resilience and stress management** written by extremely qualified experts and we are not going to be pretend to even cover the whole topic here. There is no quick fix or one-size-fits-all solution but by recognising some simple factors, hopefully it can nip in the bud some of the short-term stressors.

Symptoms of long-standing stress can be any of the following: feeling constantly tired, short tempered, uptight, distressed, depressed, paranoid and having no sense of fun. These can happen when the person affected is not actually in a stressful situation and they accept these feelings as normal. For example, they may start worrying about really trivial matters or unimportant things – every heard the phrase, "**making a mountain out of a molehill**"? That is maybe an easy way of summing it up.

Ways to help relieve stress.
There are many ways to combat stress, try some of the following:

Exercise is a great option, if you don't want to do anything strenuous, how about going for a walk? Going outdoors and getting some fresh air is a great way of clearing your head and releasing positive endorphins. It is easier on sunny day but if the weather isn't great, you can still go out on a cool crisp winter day and enjoy a walk, so don't be put off by the cold.

An old proverb says, a problem shared is a problem halved. **Talk to someone** about what it is that is stressing you out. A friend or family member. Perhaps see if they can help you put together a plan or maybe just by sharing the issue is enough to relieve some of the stress.

Try to **create a plan** to address your stress and then be realistic about how you are going to tackle it. You may need to change some things but some of those things might not be easy to change. This is where talking to someone else could be a real help.

Come to terms with things that you have no control over. Sometimes we have to **accept** that we simply have no control over somethings in life. For example, if you are working towards an exam, work project or deadline then that date is unlikely to be moved. This is where your plan comes into play and support from others will help.

If something is stressing you out, hit pause and ask yourself these questions:
  • Can I change the situation?

- Who can help me?
- What is my plan for dealing with this in the easiest possible way?

Now for the meditation.

There are many ways to meditate and we are going to start with a straightforward technique; here are the steps:

1. Find a place away from clutter and distractions.
2. Sit comfortably on a chair, cushion or the floor.
3. Close your eyes.
4. Breathe normally – in through your nose and out through your mouth.
5. Focus on your breathing – inhale for four to five seconds, exhale for five to six seconds.

Meditating for five to ten minutes a day is a great way to reduce the build-up of stress. Perhaps add some calming instrumental music.

"Wow, that was an amazing meal, where did you get that recipe from?" Mum sat back in her chair and patted her stomach in approval.

"Thea, you have a job as a full time cook now," agreed Dad. The Sunday meal was a success.

"It's all thanks to my good friend Melissa, she has been teaching me how to make some really nice meals and her dream is to be a top nutritionist and inspire other people to eat healthy, wholesome food. I would have been stressed out if it wasn't for her help."

Milo's Toolbox:
Pause before reacting to stress and assess the situation and be aware of the fight or flight situation.

Remember that most worry and stress is unnecessary.
Meditate for five to ten minutes a day.

Milo Challenges You:
Make a list of things that are stressing you out in your life at present. Are they short-term or long-term?

Now hit pause and look at the "film set".

Assess the situation and ask yourself, "would this situation still affect me in five years' time?"

Focus on the solution and not the problem.

Fun Facts – Noitatidem – that's meditation spelled backwards... now try it upside down

Meditation is a fantastic stress relief but there are also some unusual versions of this popular past time. These include Nude Yoga, yes spiritual enlightenment in the buff. Then there is aerial yoga which involves basically hanging upside down. If you love horses then you'll love equine yoga where you can find harmony through movement and breathing with a horse. Not for the quiet and relaxing types, tantrum yoga combines screaming and stretching. Sounds a bit stressful for our liking.

L is for Listen –
You Can't Listen Without Being Silent

"When you talk, you are only repeating what you already know but if you listen, you may learn something new." – Dalai Lama (Spiritual leader of the Tibetan people)

"But Sir, you didn't tell me!" Rico answered back to Mr Switchblade.

"Boy, you were the only one in the lesson who didn't complete the task. You should pay more attention; perhaps then you will start performing better."

It was an all too familiar situation in the classroom. An awkward silence fell upon the students, as challenging Mr Switchblade wasn't recommended. Rico was now being made an example of in front of everyone. Everyone else had listened of course and the instructions were clear and simple at the start of the lesson. Milo knew that Rico had been chatting to another classmate at the time but the classmate had been smart enough to ask his teacher a few questions after everyone else had begun work.

Be silent and listen.

Listening is one of the best life skills for learning; it is amazing what you can pick up by being a **great listener**. The issue is that a huge proportion of the population lack the ability to **listen** effectively, which causes breakdowns in communication across the world.

The popularity of social media is one of the reasons that has led us to believe that we need to be heard. From showing off our latest gadget, outfit or hairstyle to telling everyone what we had for dinner, we love to show off our lives. The internet is a place where most people publish their opinions from the comfort of an online status.

Research facts.

According to the **International Listening Association**, more than thirty-five of their studies showed that **listening** is the skill needed for success in business. This must be a top skill to add to our **Future Toolbox.** Less than 2% of companies actually run training courses on **listening** skills and it certainly isn't formally tested in our education system.

Have you ever watched a film with one of those really annoying people who talks all the way through it?
Ever tried to get your point across to someone but you can't get a word in edgeways?

How does this make you feel? Frustrated? Angry? Low on confidence? Imagine how others feel if they are on the receiving end of you doing this to them by not **listening** to them!

Two ears and one mouth.
The above features on our head are 2:1. Perhaps that suggests that we should do twice as much **listening** as we do talking.

We communicate through our senses; think about how we receive communications.

- Our noses receive smell.
- Our hands receive touch.
- Our eyes receive images.
- Our tongues receive taste.
- Our ears receive sound.

After our eyes, our ears receive the most signals. As soon as we open our mouths and create noise, we cut off the ability for our ears to work effectively.

So if our education system isn't going to test us on it and our companies are not going to train us on it, we need to learn this skill ourselves. Perhaps that is why teachers always tell their students to be quiet.

It is actually simple to become a master listener.
The first step is to remember that silence is golden. "**Silent**" and "**listen**" actually contain the same letters (wow) so they are even more closely linked than we realise. Perhaps they are twin brothers who work in perfect harmony.

Here's the obvious bit (yet the bit that is missed so frequently)! We need to become **silent** in order to **listen**! However, most of us are planning our response before we have finished hearing.

Now it's time to focus, concentrate on the words that you are hearing and then hit that pause button again. This is the same pause button that featured in **M is for Meditation** – we do like to give you tools that have more than one use. Hit pause for a second or two before your response.

Silence is golden, not awkward!
With practice, this pause will give you the chance to digest the information and allow your brain to settle its signal. Similar to eating

food, it is nicer to swallow one mouthful before taking the next one. That's right, savour the taste or in this case, savour the information that you have been fed.

This has opened the neural pathways in our mind (hmm, remember **O is for Open Your Mind**? There is a pattern emerging here.) You see, tools with multiple purposes!

Remember, we don't all speak the same language.
If a person from Mongolia had a conversation with a person from Comoros, they may struggle with a language barrier. (Please note, Comoros is an African island nation in the Indian Ocean between Mozambique and Madagascar and Mongolia is a landlocked country located between China and Russia. Just in case you didn't know.)

However, just because you speak the same international language as someone, it doesn't mean they will understand exactly what you are saying.

The English language is full of wonderful examples of confusion at its best.
- A roll, bap, bun, barm, cob, muffin or teacake! Seven different words for a small piece of bread, depending on what part of the country you live in.
- Bagsy, dibs or shotgun generally mean the same too, which do you prefer?
- Budge up, scoot over, move on… or chinwag, gossip, catch up, jaw-wagging, chat… the list goes on.

Spelling is there to catch us out too, how about the sound produced with words ending with OUGH?

Try these, same spelling at the end but different sound: **although** (o), **borough** (uh), **bough** (ow), **through** (oo), **cough** (off), **enough** (uf), **hiccough** (up) and **snowplough** (ow).

If that isn't enough then we have **loose, moose, goose** and **noose** all rhyming with **juice**. Many people get lose and loose mixed up too. Lose

144

means to not win and loose means not tight. However, **lose** rhymes with **whose** but doesn't thyme with **nose, hose, rose, pose** and **close** as well as **doze** and **froze**. Confusing isn't it? **Dose** doesn't rhyme with any of them. Arghhh... see below for more help!

Then we have **homophones**, words that sound the same but mean completely different things. **Pause, paws, pores, pours** – the same sound but means either to stop for a moment, something on an animal's foot, part of your anatomy or the word that follows, when it rains, it...

We have talked about hitting the **pause** button but the **paws** button wouldn't have made sense.

The **two-way communication** path has the potential to break down so remember, when you are talking, what is the **listener** is receiving? Do they understand your message? Are they giving you full attention or perhaps planning their response?

That evening at home, Milo sat on the sofa with his mum and they were chatting with her friend Peggy. Peggy had popped over to learn more about Mum's new business venture.

Ever noticed that with some people it's quite difficult to get a word in edgeways? Well that was a description of Peggy, she talked at a hundred miles an hour.

"Milo, how are your mock exams going? Your mum tells me you have been selected for some project too, how's that going? You must be proud? I bet it's good isn't it? I did something like that at work. I like those training programmes where you learn about yourself. I was told I should listen more but I dunno, I'm a pretty good listener. I used to get distracted at school as well, I bet you do sometimes, don't you?"

And breathe! Smiling politely, Milo wasn't sure what part of the question or statement to answer or comment on first. What seemed like an age but was probably about five minutes passed and Peggy was still talking.

"Anyway, I better go, I've got to get home and get dinner sorted. I'm so hungry and then I've got to get everything ready for work tomorrow. Honestly, I don't know where time goes do you? I'm always so busy all the time. Anyway, you'll have to tell me about your venture sometime when I have time…"

Hit the pause/paws/pores/pours button. **Pause** it is!
Do you need a rest too? How are Milo and his mum feeling now?

"Wow son, she can talk for England that lady," his mum said after closing the door and mopping her brow, "I'm exhausted!"

"Me too," replied Milo, as he took a deep breath out and raised his eyes into the top of his head.

They both sat back on the sofa and slumped into the back cushion. Milo grabbed his journal from the arm and they analysed what just happened.

- Peggy's sentences were dominated by I, my and me. It was clear who the focus is on.
- She asked multiple questions in one sentence but didn't pause for an answer. At times, she assumed the answer before carrying on.
- She asked questions on the following subjects: exams, projects, work, training, listening, school, dinner, work (again), busy and venture and didn't get one single piece of information from Milo or his mum.
- Finally, Peggy left without actually learning about the opportunity which was her main purpose for the visit. She had potentially missed out on learning something new.

Milo and his mum both agreed with the last statement as she wasn't going to be at the top of the list to invite again in a hurry.

The memory of Rico's telling off in class that morning was also fresh in Milo's mind. Distractions are a huge factor in us miscommunicating so now is the time to focus more.

146

Mum pointed at Thea who was sitting on the floor watching TV.

"Your sister isn't great at listening, is she?"

Breaking her gaze at the screen, Thea turned around, "Did I miss something?" she asked.

Milo's Toolbox:
Become a good listener.
Pause before reacting to speak, ask one question at a time and avoid assuming the answer.
Be careful of knee-jerk reactions.
Make a conscious (con-shus) effort to spell things correctly.

Milo Challenges You:
WIIFM versus WIIFT.

Instead of thinking about **what's in it for me**, think **what's in it for them**. Take on board the other person's point.

At times we get absorbed in ourselves and our own ego stops us from **listening** to and learning from others.

Make a note of good tips from experts, the most successful people in the world always **listen** to other people's advice.

Fun Facts – But I thought you said…
It's funny how we hear what we want to hear from time to time but sometimes we are not alone. Fancy watching the big screen? Well these

famous phrases have been said billions and billions of times but, believe it or not, some of them were never spoken!

- "**Luke, I am your father**" was not actually said by Darth Vader in *Return of the Jedi*. He actually said, **"No, I am your father"**
- Staying on the intergalactic theme, **"Beam me up Scotty!"** was thought to have been said by Captain James T Kirk in the original *Star Trek* but the closest he ever came was **"Scotty, beam me up."**
- Never ever has Sherlock Holmes said the words, **"Elementary, my dear Watson!"** This quote was written in a film review in the *New York Times* on October 19, 1929.

A friend from years ago started dating a rich guy who asked her what she would like for Christmas, so she asked him for a sports car. On Christmas Day, she awoke to open a smaller than expected gift which was shaped like a box. Ah perhaps the keys were inside. Peeling back the wrapping paper, she discovered it was a foot spa. Oh well, at least she could relax her feet!

Spelling and word help.
Confusing but fascinating, that's the English language. We must always respect and love it so why not pay attention to **spelling and grammar**? A great life skill to put into your **Future Toolbox** is to add to your vocabulary as often as you can. We've certainly learnt some new words and phrases whilst writing this book.

The OUGH words:
- **Although** (o) – regardless of the fact that; even though: *Although the room is big, it won't hold all that furniture.*
- **Borough** (uh) – a self-governing incorporated town: *The Borough of Northampton.*
- **Bough** (ow) – a large or main tree branch: *When the bough breaks, the cradle will fall…* *
- **Through** (oo) – Moving in one side and out of the other side of: *Look through the window.*
- **Cough** (off) – Expel air from the lungs with a sudden sharp sound: *He tried to speak and started to cough.*

- **Enough** (uf) – As much or as many as required: *I've had enough food.*
- **Hiccough** (up) – An involuntary spasm of the diaphragm and respiratory organs, with a sudden closure of the glottis and a characteristic gulping sound: *She has hiccoughs.*
- **Snowplough** (ow) – A vehicle for clearing roads of thick snow by pushing it aside: *The weather was so bad that the snowplough was deployed.*

The confusing rhyming and non-rhyming words.
- **Loose** – opposite to tight.
- **Moose** – a big animal that can be found in Canada, for example.
- **Goose** – a large water bird that doesn't actually lay golden eggs.
- **Noose** – a type of knot which tightens when pulled.
- **Juice** – the liquid from a fruit such as an orange, for example.
- **Lose** – the opposite win.
- **Whose** – a belonging associated to which person.
- **Nose** – that thing in the middle of your face designed for smelling things with.
- **Hose** – a pipe that a liquid is fed along, water, for example.
- **Rose** – a flower.
- **Pose** – pretend to be, show off or put yourself in a position to be photographed, for example.
- **Close** – opposite to open or it could be the opposite to not far away (that would be another rhyme).
- **Doze** – a light sleep.
- **Froze** – the past tense of to freeze.
- **Dose** – a quantity of something to be taken, medicine, for example.

* Don't forget that **bough** (as in the tree branch) also rhymes with **bow** (an action that you may perform in front or a queen or king) but **bow** (as in bow and arrow is also spelt the same). We could go on forever but, you see, the English language is fascinating. Enjoy it!

K is for Kiss – Kiss and Make Up

"Trade your expectations for appreciation and your whole world changes in an instant." – Tony Robbins (author, entrepreneur, philanthropist and life coach)

Don't you just hate it when people say they hate things? OK detect the irony there! Hate is a pretty strong word though and it's said at will by people of all ages.

Young children will tell their mum or dad, "I hate you," when they don't get their own way. They probably don't really mean it and are too naive to realise what they are saying. This then becomes a negative habit.

Go on, make a mental note over the next week how many times people say they hate something. Include the amount of times you say it too. You will be shocked.

The *Oxford English Dictionary* definition of hate is to, "Have an intense dislike of."

Perhaps we dislike certain things but do we really need to fill our life with so much so-called hate? The word is used flippantly a lot of the time and could probably be avoided.

For example, "I hate algebra," may actually mean, "I don't understand algebra!" Perhaps, "I hate squid," may actually mean, "I have yet to try squid... I do not know how it tastes but I am not prepared to try it yet!" "I hate rain," probably means that it is not your favourite type of weather. Anyway, we talked earlier about the things you can't control so why do we spend so much time getting down about it? I mean, we need water to live and it falls from the sky so perhaps we need to get over it and accept that it is something of beauty in the phenomenon of our world.

Wow, perhaps the **mindsets** are being preconceived to condition ourselves to create a negative view of something we don't really appreciate.

Now we are not going to be in love with absolutely everything we see, do or experience in life but perhaps we can lose some of the negative hate we build in our life.

Try and cut the word from your vocabulary by at least half and replace it with, "I'm not sure of...", "I'm not so keen on..." or "That's not for me". How about even opening your mind and look at your view from another angle?

Lose the Spite.
Earlier on we mentioned that the world is dominated by bad news and the knock-on effect is for many individuals to jump on the bandwagon of spite and hatred.

Social media is also a place which attracts spite and hatred at times. As already mentioned, some individuals seem comfortable to hide behind a screen and air their views to the world. Sadly, this is damaging to themselves as much as the person or organisation they are offending.

I met up with a high-profile individual recently (you would know his name but I will not reveal him to you). He was victim of a news story that made national headlines but was made up by a bitter and twisted associate of his. The associate had basically stirred a rumour about his private life in order to cause some damage to his profile and when a newspaper heard this, they decided to run it as a story. The story wasn't true of course and, after spending months and money trying to clear his name, he decided to fight fire with fire and produce his own statement in the media with the truth. It worked and he was able to sue the associate and the newspaper for the damage it caused to his reputation. He wasn't interested in making any money from the case so he donated the full amount to charity.

The initial report was a pretty lame statement and escalated out of control due to his fame and ended up causing a lot of upset to him and his children but some people in the world revelled in his downfall.

This chap is a really caring person and if you were to meet him, you would struggle not to like or respect him and his values but many people's ignorance cast a different view from afar.

Whether you are the reader or the source of the spiteful statements, be careful. It will cause too much damage to too many!

How many times do you say something about someone or even spread a rumour that may not be true. Gossip is horrible to the person on the receiving end of these bullying statements. Sometimes even innocent comments can be taken the wrong way or what seems like a bit of fun may not be received well. Think before you speak. There is a fine line between banter and bullying.

It was time to take on the "Hate challenge!" Milo began counting how many times he had said he hated things that day. He hated a

song on the radio, hated a subject at school, hated a jacket that a friend was wearing and the food they were eating for lunch.

Dad hit three within minutes of sitting at the dinner table: he hated the traffic that morning, the torrential downpour that got him wet whilst going into the office and the parking warden who almost gave him a ticket.

Mum only hit one and that was saying she hates it when Dad moans. "That warden was only doing his job you know and you were fifteen minutes over the time of your ticket. He did wait for you and not give you a ticket after all!"

Thea was winning hands down by halfway through the meal. She hated drama because she didn't get selected for the role that she wanted. She hated the group for not selecting her. She hated her friend Melissa for getting the role and her drama teacher for giving it to Melissa, and also hated her costume. She also hated life for being unfair.

If six wasn't enough, she also added on hating the rain that day even though she was inside when it came down and she also expressed hate for the bus driver for no apparent reason. It appeared to have been a bad day for her as she pushed her fork around the plate whilst resting her chin on her other hand. All of the comments may have been quite flippant and she probably didn't really actually mean them. They had certainly made her feel pretty down though and it was going to be hard to pick herself up and move onto the next chapter of the day now.

These examples have also been caused by a series of scenarios from mainly uncontrollable events including jealousy to her friend, resentment to her teacher, opinions of others, self confidence and then there is the weather which we definitely can't change.

The family attempted to lift her spirits and instil a bit of positivity back into her as they continued eating.

"Hey, look, you did your best to get the part," Dad said smiling. "Melissa will be great at it and you will get another chance anyway!"

Mum tried a similar tactic, "Yeah, sometimes things aren't meant to be and this will help you come back even stronger next time!"

Finally, Milo remembered what he had been reading in his latest chapter:

It is time to kiss and make up.
In a similar manner to most of our life skills, we can combine many tools from our **Future Toolbox** to combat the negativity caused.

O is for Open Your Mind – try to flip the positives into negatives. Perhaps his sister could have been pleased for Melissa getting the part and embraced what it meant to her.

L is for Listen – next she could ask Melissa for advice on how she got the part and learn from her audition and how she performed. Look at her success habits.

The resentment and jealousy, or hate as she referred to in this instance, could be lifted and she can move on with her life.

Dad hated the traffic and the weather plus the warden. Not many people are going to fall in love with being stuck in the traffic of course but how about embracing the time in the car and listening to some of your favourite music or even better, an inspirational story or motivational audio.

The rain will fall on us all, clean our street and feed nature. As for the traffic warden, Dad could have used the tool **S is for Smile** and appreciated not getting a ticket while saying thank you as a gesture from a decent human being for giving him that extra minute and avoiding the fine. The laws of attraction and karma work in strange and powerful ways. Perhaps that warden would remember the friendly gesture the next time he sees a car parked slightly over the time allowed. So, can we "kiss and make up" with our friends, the traffic, the weather and the laws? Open your mind and try it, you will actually find that most people are pretty decent.

The after-dinner chatter turned into laughter as everyone realised that life was actually pretty good. As they all went to leave the table, Mum positively asked "OK, who loves the washing up?"

Future Toolbox

Milo's Toolbox:

Create more positivity in my world by eliminating hate where possible.

Remember not to try and control the things that we can't control.

Be genuinely pleased for others who achieve.

Milo Challenges You:

We talked about a world that builds dramatisation of hate through the media and television. Continue living in your world not the world by avoiding negative conversation where possible.

Count up the times that you say the word hate or where you notice people trying to put others down. Try to give people praise and be inspired by their success.

Add hate to the list of negative words to cut out of my daily vocabulary – avoid *I hate, I can't, I won't and I don't know* where possible.

Fun facts – Love is strange

Love is a funny thing and can lead to the strangest romantic gestures. Ben Affleck and Jennifer Lopez were one of Hollywood's most talked about couples in the early 2000s. Ben spent $105,000 on a toilet seat covered in rare gems including diamonds, rubies, and sapphires. Nothing says I love you like a toilet seat.

Married on his hundredth birthday after chasing her for thirty years.
This is a love story that money can't buy though. In 1983, a seventy-two-year-old called Forrest Lunsway went on a blind date with sixty-two-year-old Rose Pollard. Rose said that she only wanted to be friends but Forrest wouldn't give up. Over the next twenty years, he consistently drove the forty miles back and forth between their homes just so he could see her again. In 2003 he proposed to her and she joked that if he lived to be 100 she would marry him. Well, in 2011 – when she was ninety and on the day he turned 100 – they finally got married.

What would you give up for love? Edward VIII became King of England in 1936 but later that year he proposed to a married American woman named Wallis Simpson. Royalty would not allow him to see her whilst he was king so he was given the choice – choose between her or his throne. He chose her. She divorced her husband and they were married the next year. It shows that money and fame isn't everything.

J is for Job Satisfaction – Love What You Do

"Choose a job you love and never work a day in your life." –
Confucius (Chinese philosopher)

There he stood in front of the mirror straightening his tie and
adjusting his jacket. "Looking good," he thought to himself as he
admired his reflection. How was he feeling? Nervous? Certainly!
Excited? A little! Prepared? As ready as he could be!

Milo had handed in an application form to the local coffee shop
last week after seeing an advert in the shop window. He knew the
assistant manager as he regularly visited the shop, instead of
Father Russmuss's Food Box, with his mates on the way home
from school or at weekends when they used it as a hangout for

chatter or sometimes study. It was a lovely relaxing environment but the biggest pull for them all was the amazing homemade cakes on sale.

First Impressions Last.
We only ever get one shot at the first impression and Milo's first success was always being polite and smiling as a customer when visiting. On the day he collected the application form, he went into the shop on his own and dressed smartly. After completing it, in his best handwriting, he made another visit to hand it to the owner personally. This must have worked because his phone rang the following day with the offer of an interview. As the saying goes, the rest is history.

It was Wednesday after school and he had rushed home and changed into his interview gear. So, here he stood in his suit ready to go. In his pocket was a small notebook with some prepared questions in it.

- Who are the team that I'll be working with?
- What training will I get?
- What are the best and worst parts of the job?

Simple questions but effective, straight to the point and most importantly – planned. The interview was at 5 p.m. so he quickly read his notes again, checked himself in the mirror and left the house. Wandering down the street, Milo was keen to get this part-time job and thought about what he could learn here. He knew his long-term career goal wasn't working in a coffee shop but what life skills could he gain?

Communication, confidence, responsibility from handling money, basic numeracy from counting change and customer service skills.

A quick glance at the watch, the time was 4:51 p.m. and time to enter the shop for the interview. The bell dinged on the door and the smiling lad called Ethan Espresso greeted him from behind the counter, "Hello, can I help you mate?"

"Good afternoon, I have an interview with Lois Latte," he said, professionally, confidently and with a smile.

The lad walked around the front of the counter and took Milo through to Lois's office at the back of the shop. She was finishing a phone call but glanced up and smiled a huge, welcoming smile and beckoned him to take a seat. The office was compact with a small, neat tidy desk and just enough room for a chair either side.

Lois finished the call, put down the phone and stood up to greet Milo. He responded by standing and offering a handshake and confidently greeting her, "Good afternoon Lois, I'm really pleased to meet you and thank you for seeing me today."

Suddenly his nerves seemed to disappear as they both began chatting. It seemed like more of a conversation instead of an interview. Lois did ask some questions but the answers seemed to roll off the tongue as Milo used a technique he was taught by Naomi, a careers adviser at school.

Use a **feature** and a **benefit** to really sell your strengths and personality to the interviewer was the advice. The **feature** is what it does and the **benefit** is what it gives, so make that personal to you.

"I'm proud to have been selected for a life skills programme called Future Toolbox" – **feature**

"This has allowed me to improve my confidence, communication skills and become an all-round positive person" – benefit (wow, what an answer).

Lois's responses were positive and as the interview drew to a close, she said, "Well I think you have certainly answered everything I need but do you have any final questions for me?"

He pulled the small notebook from his pocket, opened it and summarised the prepared questions, "Well I was going to ask about the training but you said that I will get a chance to do on the job training plus a Barista qualification too. That sounds fantastic! Also, you answered my question about the team. Of course, I have met them in person but you said about the small, family-run business and everyone is really friendly here. I like that and think I'll fit in really well. Ethan Espresso has served me many times in the shop and always chats to me when I pop in to do some study, you know, study when you want to get away from distractions at home?"

Wow, name dropping Ethan Espresso, who worked in the shop, and also showing that he is keen to study as well, this has to be like gold dust in the interview.

Nodding with approval, Lois was clearly impressed that he didn't just answer, no I have nothing to add. She explained that she was going to make a decision as soon as possible.

"I won't keep you waiting long and hopefully you can start on Saturday as we discussed."

"Thank you so much for the opportunity today and just to let you know, the job sounds brilliant, I'm really keen and look forward to hearing from you soon." Milo shook hands and left the interview with his head held high. He was almost skipping down the high street, feeling very proud, start Saturday, that sounded like it would be good news.

Why get a job? Work to learn and not to earn.
Naturally we need to earn money to pay for the necessities in life: rent/mortgage, bills, food, clothes plus nice things too. What are the most important things to employees in their jobs?

A **Future Toolbox** survey asked apprentices (who had been employed between six and twelve months), what is the most important thing to you in your job and here are their results:
1. Job satisfaction.
2. Responsibilities.
3. The people and the team.

4. Money.
5. Where the job will lead to.

We also surveyed experienced workers who had been in employment for over five years and guess what? Yep, similar answers. Self-employed business owners gave the same top answer too – **job satisfaction.**

Enjoy the ride.
The majority of people who work full time will spend around a third of their life at work. We know that from **Z is for ZZZ** that we spend on average a third of our life sleeping, it should be around eight to ten hours per night. That leaves us a third for ourselves. **T is for Time** taught us about time and how much of it we can waste.

So why do so many people have a job or career that they don't enjoy? They spend so much time doing it, right?

Let's look at the time factor a little more in-depth.
Eight hours sleep, eight hours at work… there is sixteen hours gone. The remaining eight could be spent as such:
- One hour getting ready for work.
- One hour getting to work.
- One hour getting home.
- We now have five hours left… maybe another hour could be spend dreading the following day whilst preparing for it.
- Four hours left and time is ticking away… and some people will spend a lot of that time watching TV or on a mobile device.

Live for the weekend.
If this person, for example, works Monday to Friday, then they have their weekends free. That's two whole days to themselves. Ratios mean that you get two out of every seven days to yourselves to enjoy, which would equal two out of every seven years or even more scarily, twenty out of seventy years. Would you choose to waste fifty years of your life doing something you don't enjoy?

It's a shame but so many people get caught in the trap known as the rat race, working for a boss they don't necessarily like, a company who sets

161

rules they may not agree with, has morals that could go against their values. Even some business owners say the hardest boss to work for is themselves as they can't walk away from their work and switch off at the end of the day. Our education system has rules telling us what time to be at school, what time to go home, when to take a break, what to wear, when we can talk and when we can go to the toilet. It certainly makes a school an easier place to run but the human race then becomes used to being told what to do.

"I never did a day's work in my life. It was all fun." – Thomas Edison (inventor and businessman)

The above may have sounded a little depressing, so how do we make work fun like Thomas Edison did? Firstly, we have to respect the rules of course. Sometimes we spend too much energy changing the things we can't change but not enough energy changing ourselves or our situation.

In our **Future Toolbox** MAD4Study sessions, we show students ways to make revision and study easy and fun by using mind maps, stories and journeys with strange and memorable associations. If you're having fun then you are more likely to want to perform the task and ultimately be successful.

Work to learn, not to earn.
Anyone who has been employed will tell you that learning a new job role is tiring as there is so much to take in. Whatever your path in life, having a job and working for someone is a really good way to build a foundation for the future. OK, you get paid at work but why not be hungry to learn as well? Even if it isn't a dream job or a little boring, find out what you are doing and why you are doing it. How does this fit into the process of the company? This will help you to find out your purpose. Offer to do more, you never know, it may open a door of opportunity.

In my first ever job at a building society (the one I walked two miles to every day), my responsibility was to sort mortgage statements. I was told to match a figure on a statement to a figure on a printout from the computer. If they matched then the statement went in an envelope and was sent to the customer and if it didn't, I had to perform a simple calculation and send it to Sheila on table twelve. Sounds very boring doesn't it? However, after a few weeks, I decided to go and talk to Sheila and find out what she did with the calculation and she explained it to me. I won't bore you with the details but suddenly I understood the point of my job and realised that I had a purpose. The more questions I asked, the more I learnt. The more I learnt, the more responsibilities I got. After three months I was called into the manager's office and given a new role, it was like a mini promotion and awarded not one but two pay rises. Yes, two pay rises. The manager said how impressed she was that I asked lots of questions and was really willing to learn. Imagine I had turned my nose up and complained from week one, regularly telling everyone how boring the job was. Instead, I worked to learn and ended up earning more anyway. It was win–win.

Value to the market place.
Business philosopher, Jim Rohn, summed up how employment works. Simple, you are paid to bring value to the market place. For example, if you are paid minimum wage, it means that your job role adds minimum value to the market place, it doesn't mean that you are worth minimum value personally. If you work hard and add more to your role then you become worth more and may be paid more. If not, then it may be time to move on.

For example, if the top director of a company brings in £100bn of revenue a year then would they be worth a salary of £5m a year? Well they are certainly bringing value to the market place so perhaps the answer would be yes.

Mr Rohn also said "Learn all you can and dump what you don't need later!" This is a little like the story of our mature student friend in **O is for Open Your Mind**. She was willing to write down everything that the lecturer at university gave her instead of asking if the information would appear in the exam.

A job is not a job for life.
According to recent studies, how many **career changes** does a person have in their working life? The answer is **seven**. That number is predicted to rise quite substantially too.

Further studies show that some graduates are beginning degrees that will be out of date by the time they graduate. St Andrews University stated that technology is replacing jobs at the highest rate ever.

Back in the 1980s, cars were made by people but production line robots were introduced. Workers were still present on site but today, robots dominate the manufacturing process. Even a car parks itself now leaving the driver to sit back in their seat after pressing a button.

People used to only shop on the high street with cash and buying something online was unheard of. Now the huge proportion of purchases are made online and money is paid electronically with the touch of a card or smartphone.

According to *Forbes Magazine*, dream jobs of children at primary school age includes being a supermodel, a spy, a ballerina or a dancer. The imagination of kids is amazing, even a job of a superhero is one of the most popular career choices. Spider-Man, Superman or Batman had better watch out. OK, maybe these jobs are a little beyond possibility but how about regular jobs? A firefighter, lawyer, police officer, doctor or astronaut are high up the list. You won't be surprised to learn that there were a lot of mentions for fame and fortune in wanting to be an actor, DJ, footballer or pop star.

Favourite jobs of teens include a YouTuber or Blogger. Will these "jobs" be around in ten years' time? Time will change, the career path a teen chooses today may change drastically with it and the company or industry may not exist in the near future.

Social media is a great example. In 2000 a couple called Steve and Julie Pankhurst launched a website called Friends Reunited and it exploded into life, within a couple of years it had over three million members. The idea of the site was to connect with friends from all over the world. Erm, isn't this like Facebook? Yes, it was four years before Facebook was launched. But, even when Facebook was launched in 2004, it wasn't the biggest social media platform, people preferred MySpace and that was the most popular social media platform until 2010. A lot of people reading this will say, Friends what? MySpace?

Back to the subject of work! Some graduates starting their degrees this year may already be studying material that is out of date. We just need to be aware of this and open our mind to the fast-changing world.

"Choose a job you love and never work a day in your life."
Let's go back to keeping it simple. We started with this quote so let's close with it. Find something you love doing and get someone to pay you for it.

How? OK, if you love cooking for instance, how can you get paid for preparing meals? If you love sport or fitness, find a way to be financially rewarded for training. Your passion is art, music, talking to people, making clothes, travel… whatever the subject, it's time to open your mind and think of some ideas. We have friends who do what they love and run businesses cooking food, painting murals, graphic design and as personal trainers. Maybe it isn't possible to be a superhero but Stan Lee and Steve Ditko were the guys who created Spiderman. Perhaps being a cartoonist is a harder career to find than say an office worker but there is no problem in dreaming big and who said that everything has to be an easy target?

Make a list of these ideas. Study people who have been paid in these areas before. Be brave and be realistic. You may not become rich immediately or even make anything at all. Be passionate, be patient and remember, like everything, it requires effort. Even if it ends up becoming just a hobby and you don't make a single penny from it, at least you have enjoyed the journey.

Ring, ring. Milo's phone buzzed later that evening.

"Hi Milo, this is Lois here, can you start on Saturday? I would like to offer you the job."

"Wow, thank you," was his excited reply.

Milo was ready to learn from his new job with Lois Latte's coffee shop.

Milo's Toolbox:
Work to learn and be keen and willing.
Ask lots of questions and find out why your job is important.
Embrace the life skills I can learn from work for the future. learn everything, not just the minimum.

Milo Challenges You:
Look at your work-life balance.

Do you enjoy what you do? Do you get paid for the value you bring to the market place?

Perhaps you are well paid but don't have any time to yourself to enjoy.

Be brave and make plans for change if you need to change.
Write down a list of things that you really enjoy and research if there is a way to get paid for them.

Fun Facts – Looking for a job with a difference? Try these...
These certainly will be a talking point at a party. Imagine meeting someone and asking what they do for a living and they reply, "I'm a Duck Master." Yep, some hotels actually hire people to take care of the ducks in their pond and occasionally walk them around the grounds.

If you like fishing or cycling (or both) then perhaps you could be a Bicycle Fisher in Amsterdam. This city is bicycle capital of the world. It's no shock to learn that a lot of these two-wheelers end up in one of the canals and the Bicycle Fishers fish out around 14,000 rusty bikes from its waterways every year.

Talking of water, why not become a Golf Ball Diver and search for the lost golf balls in the water hazards of the world's golf courses. Thousands of balls can be collected by a golf ball diver every day.

If you like your food and you love your animals then perhaps you could combine the two and become a Pet Food Tester. We'll let you guess what this involves.

Maybe your life is so exciting that you need to calm down those days and become a Drying Paint Watcher. Amazingly someone is actually paid to watch paint dry. This UK-based job involves painting sheets of cardboard to test how long new paint mixtures take to dry.

There are many more weird and wonderful professions but we'll squeeze one last one in. It's a Train Pusher (or "Oshiyas") in Japan. These are hired to help cram as many people onto a train as possible by pushing them from the outside until the doors will close.

I is for "I Am the Greatest" – Affirmations

"I am the greatest." – Muhammad Ali (professional boxer, activist, and philanthropist)

"Father–son night," Milo's dad said cupping his hands together behind his head as he relaxed back into the sofa. He grabbed the television remote and hit the on button.

Milo had been reading a chapter on inspirational people in his book and his dad had recently finished a book on world famous boxer Muhammad Ali. It seemed fitting for them to watch a documentary about Ali on the television.

The programme began.

World famous boxer Muhammad Ali had many great phrases. He would stand in front of a mirror and say, **"I am the greatest!"**

- He would appear on television and say, **"I am the greatest!"**
- In a newspaper interview he would quote, **"I am the greatest!"**
- In a pre-fight press conference he would say, **"I am the greatest!"**
- In the ring he would say to his opponent, **"I am the greatest!"**

Guess what, Muhammad Ali was the greatest boxer of his time.

He didn't stand there and say, "Well perhaps one day I might be alright!"

He words were said with conviction, posture and belief. **"I am the greatest!"** went on to be one of his most famous phrases but to Muhammad Ali, this was an **affirmation** that gave him self-belief that one day he would be a champion.

Ali went on to be the youngest world champion at the time, aged twenty-two but it wasn't all plain sailing. He had to overcome many obstacles, one being the colour of his skin.

After winning a gold medal at the Rome Olympics, he returned to his home town in Kentucky only to be refused entry to a restaurant because he was black. Wearing the gold medal around his neck at the time, he took it off and threw it into the Ohio River. He felt downhearted, having won this medal for his country but not being able to walk free without prejudice in his home town.

The American Government also stripped him of his world titles and took away his fight permit after he refused to be drafted into the U.S. Military and have any involvement in the Vietnam War in 1967. He didn't believe in war due to his religious beliefs and took legal action. After a four-year long battle of lost court cases, he finally won his rights back at the Supreme Court.

In later life, he battled Parkinson's Disease but still travelled the world raising millions of pounds for charity. Despite all these knockbacks and challenges, he maintained the phrase, **"I am the greatest!"**

"I am the greatest" is probably one of the most famous and well know **affirmations** in the world.

What is an affirmation?

Do you hear voices inside your head? Some people think that they need severe help if they do and run to call the doctor but we're going to ask you that question again – Do you hear voices inside your head? Some people sat back and thought, "No I don't hear voices inside my head, I told you I'm not mad or weird or strange…" Aha, if you did that, that is the voice inside your head telling you that you don't have a voice inside your head. Get it?

Studies show that we hear over 50,000 messages every day from ourselves. Yes, from us, not someone else. We have between 150-300 words per minute being processed by our brains. A lot of those messages are telling us how to react and it could be something like no don't or yes do. In **U is for U Can Do It** we talked about "Silence the I can't." An affirmation is a great way of doing this, add some to your **Future Toolbox**.

An **affirmation** helps to install positive thoughts into your mindset, so repeating these words to yourself, out loud or in front of others (when appropriate) helps to increase your self-belief.

"Erm, what shall I say then?"

You haven't got to psych someone out here and we don't want to sound too much like a big head or an arrogant person so we will start simple.

Also discussed in **U is for U Can Do It**, how about picking something you want to improve on. If you are not good at maths, then you could start with: "I am getting better at maths!"

Or how about, "I am going to pass my maths test!"

Try it.

An **affirmation** has to be in positive language – you cannot say, "I am not going to fail at maths" or "I might pass my maths."

Well done. The next step is to try it out. Follow these simple steps:

1. Stand in front of a mirror and look at yourself.
2. Now say your **affirmation** out loud.
3. Repeat it but say it a little louder than the first time.
4. Do it again but a little louder.
5. Repeat louder again.
6. And again.

How did that feel? Strange! A little weird! Things always do the first time but like anything, you have to practise. Repeat this process every day, keep repeating your **affirmation** and why not create new ones.

Positive thought and feelings become commands and eventually this will help you achieve what you want.
"I am the greatest!" – tell yourself it every day.

Muhammad Ali would say that phrase over and over again but here are some other possible **affirmations** that you could use:

- I am the architect of my life; I build its foundation and choose its contents.
- Today, I am full of energy and overflowing with joy.
- I have been given endless talents which I begin to use today.
- I forgive those who have harmed me in my past and peacefully detach from them.
- Happiness is a choice. I am going to be happy.
- I am courageous and I will stand up for myself.
- My thoughts are filled with positivity.
- I am blessed with an incredible family and wonderful friends.
- I am a powerhouse and I am indestructible.
- I have beauty, charm, and grace.

As the programme's credits rolled up the screen on the television, Milo turned to his dad.

"We are the greatest!"

They high fived each other!

Milo's Toolbox:
Use positive language to build my self-belief·
Stick to my beliefs and truly believe in myself·
Use my affirmation first thing in the morning and last thing at night· The more times I repeat it the more positive I will become and the stronger I will feel·

Milo Challenges You:
Create and use your positive **affirmation**(s) on a daily basis. Try printing and framing the words and place them somewhere where you can see them all the time. Read them aloud whenever you pass the frame. This will instil positivity into your daily life.

Fun Facts – The power of words
Affirmations can be so powerful that it is a good tip to display them somewhere where you can see them every day. Some people are committed to those words that they will bind them to themselves by getting them tattooed to their bodies. We called this book, ***Don't Get Your Neck Tattooed*** for a reason but perhaps you shouldn't get a tattoo at all. Here is a collection of tattoos gone horribly wrong:

- Never don't give up – erm, this was tattooed on a person's leg. Make sure you say the words out loud before committing to ink.
- FEAR LES ♥ – a guy had this tattooed on each of his fingers but who is Les and should he be feared?
- A bloke who wanted the Chinese symbols for "Live and let live" on his arm ended up with the Mandarin for "Sweet and Sour Chicken". Tasty.
- A man had "Jenius" inked on his forehead, instead of "genius". Not such a genius thing to do, eh?

- A woman who used an internet translation tool to translate "I love David" into Hebrew later discovered the phrase actually translated into "Babylon is the world's leading dictionary and translation software."
- Another unlucky woman wanted her favourite flower name written across her lower back but was left with "Sweet Pee" above her waistline.
- A mum decided to show tribute to her daughter by inking her initials in Mandarin. Unfortunately the characters actually mean: 所 place, 狗 dog.
- A girl got a tattoo on her arm and thought it said "beautiful" in Mandarin, but it actually said "calamity, disaster, catastrophe."

H is for Habits – Create Positive Habits

"You are what you repeatedly do. Excellence is then not an act, it's a habit." – Will Durant (American writer, historian, and philosopher)

Hands up if you have a bad habit!

If you didn't put your hand up then are probably not being entirely truthful, are you?

According to *The Huffington Post* the most annoying habits in the world include:

- Talking loudly on the phone or using speaker phone.
- Sharing TMI (too much information) about personal things.

- Asking for help with the same problems again and again, instead of simply taking the time to learn to do it properly.
- Being late.
- Leaving your mess behind and expecting someone else to clean up.
- Posting cryptic messages on social media, instead of just speaking to someone about the issue.
- Gossiping about everyone and everything around.
- Listening to music loudly or – worse – singing and whistling along.
- Eating really loud or chewing with your mouth open.
- Leaving your phone notifications dinging and pinging all day long.
- Not taking responsibility for mistakes – or worse, blaming others.

When we talk about bad habits in **Future Toolbox** sessions with teenagers or adults, these are the top bad habits that people admit to in the room.
- Biting nails.
- Clicking or cracking your fingers.
- Being late.
- Interrupting people.
- Smoking.
- Procrastinating.
- Spending too much time on my phone or electronic device.
- Eating too much junk food or skipping meals.

Do you possess any of these habits on a daily basis?

How to change a bad habit.
OK, there are going to be a few steps to changing a bad habit but first…

Warning, warning, this is not going to be easy!

We are going to take on the thirty-day challenge. Now there is no science behind the timescale, some experts will say thirty days, some will say 3,000 repetitions but regardless of this, around a month is a good benchmark top make the change.

Preparation Stage 1 – Commitment and announcement.
OK, here we go. The first step is to make a commitment to yourself. Nobody else can do it for you. How about making an announcement to someone else that you are going to break this habit? By making the news public, it means someone else can support you and help you stay. Ask them to give you a friendly reminder if they notice you going off track.

Milo looked at the ends of his fingers. His nails were rugged from the constant biting of his nails. He thought to himself about how much this habit annoys people with him. Fidelma kept telling him to stop biting whilst they were studying together the previous day and Mum is constantly telling him off at home too. He was now serious and decided to start with his affirmation.

"I will stop biting my nails," he announced aloud. After pausing, he thought about positive language. "Erm, my nails are growing…" he giggled to himself. "Yep, that'll will do," he decided.

Popping downstairs to his parents, he announced, "I'm going to stop biting my nails, if you see me biting them, will you make me aware? Nicely that is."

Step one – Days 1-10: The really painful and unbearable stage.
Warning, warning, this is where most people quit!

After making your commitment and announcing it to the world, this stage is going to be horrible and extremely hard. You will want to give up, consciously and subconsciously, and want to go back to your old ways. If those people supporting you and constantly reminding you that you are slipping up, it could make you feel negative about yourself and even as if you are failing. You must dig in and **show true grit** here and whatever you do, you mustn't snap at the people supporting you.

It was absolute torture at the start. His hands always automatically moved towards his teeth to chomp on those nails. Milo's subconscious mind was in overdrive, he had created and followed this habit for many years and was usually completely unaware he was doing it.

Every time someone reminded him that he was breaking the habit, he felt frustrated but he knew he was committed. He held his tongue and wouldn't snap back.

Step two – Days 11-20: The uncomfortable stage.
Congratulations if you have made it to this stage. Over a week and a half, you have now been sticking to your goal and well on your way to success. It is still **going to be tough** and there is a lot of work to do. Beware of being tempted to take a day off but if you do this, you are effectively going back to day one and having to start again. Stick with it and **keep digging in**.

"Our greatest weakness lies in giving up. The most certain way to succeed is always to try just one more time." – Thomas Edison (inventor and businessman)

When Milo makes it to this stage, there should be no going back now, his nails will be starting to grow and look better already. He will slip up at times but then become instantly aware that he was about to put his fingers in his mouth. The conscious mind will now be starting to take over.

Step three – Days 21-30: The unstoppable stage.
You have now reached the stage where you are more **in control** of your habit and it no longer owns you. You are conscious of your actions and you have most likely replaced a bad habit with a **positive one**. In this stage, it is all about maintenance and making sure you don't slip back to your old ways.

More warnings. Crossing the finish line isn't always the end of the race. Use your positive success to create a new goal and kick another bad habit. We have seen friends become the new them, hit a little plateau and then go back to the old them. A weight loss diet or fitness plan for example, a particular friend of ours wanted to get fit and lose a few stone in weight. She worked tirelessly on cutting out highly processed foods and replacing the sofa with the gym. After reaching her target weight, she stopped going to the gym and began eating junk food again. It took only half the time to return to her original weight but this time she felt twice as unhappy. You will be pleased to know that she did begin a new healthy lifestyle plan to get herself back to fitness again.

One thing to consider is that it will be hard but remember, once you get past the unstoppable stage you have to stay in the maintenance stage to ensure that you don't slip right back to the start. The successful people in life are those who are prepared to do the things unsuccessful people aren't prepared to do.

His habit will be beaten if Milo can get to this stage. Back to the present day, he closed his eyes and visualised himself standing proudly above a slayed lion. His fingertips looked healthier and he was now using a nail clipper every week to trim them. His fingers were no longer feeling painful but the biggest difference he noticed, people around him were no longer irritated by his old habit too. Now the long hard slog of breaking the habit must begin.

Affirmation + habit = success.
Adding affirmations whilst working towards your habits will help you to stay on track towards achieving your goal. Back to our friend who is now on track with her fitness and healthy lifestyle plan again, her goal is to lose around two stone, be active and have more energy.

Firstly, she looked at her habits and realised that one of her biggest downfalls was eating too many biscuits and crisps. She decided to replace these unhealthy snacks with a piece of fruit, a handful of nuts and seeds or a rice cake. Also, instead of fizzy drinks, she drank water infused with fresh lemon or strawberry to add some sweetness to her drink. Next, she added a positive affirmation. Instead of constantly saying, "I am trying to lose weight," her statement was, "I now weigh xx kilos." She would repeat this affirmation to herself every day, especially at meal times and whilst she was exercising or working out. She achieved her goal in around three months and plans to maintain her newly-created habits.

If Milo's affirmation was, "I am going to stop biting my nails," his brain would hear the words biting my nails. The laws of attraction would kick in and have a strong power-play on the mind. The brain would then focus on biting my nails. Your strongest thoughts and feelings become commands and this mixed message to the brain will confuse it. If your willpower is low, the focus ends up swinging towards what you don't want. In this case, Milo will probably end up biting his nails. How about this affirmation instead? "My nails are healthy!"

Here are some examples of good affirmations:
- I am smoke free.
- I weight xx kilos.
- I have saved £500.
- I am punctual and prepared.
- I am calm, relaxed and stress free.

Not all habits are bad.
We all focus on the bad habits we possess but how about the good ones?

He has now started his new job and Milo looked at his contract that Lois Latte gave him, outlining his job details including hours and salary. He decided to start a new habit. After reading W is for Wonga again, every week when he gets paid, Milo is going to put 10% of his earnings into a savings account. Imagine what investment he will have for the future.

Study the good habits for success.
Why not study the habits of successful people? Business people make those few extra business calls or contacts. Think about who these people study too. How did they become successful? Perhaps there is a classmate or someone at school, college or university who seems to pass tests easily or get great grades. What do they do? Where do they study? What plans do they have in place? Ask successful people for their top three tips on how they became successful.

179

Maybe start a new exercise habit or healthier eating plan of your own. Walk or jog around the block or the park every day or try a new type of health food.

Habit hooking.
Milo read the final section of this chapter, it says; A great and simple way to create a new habit is by hooking it to an existing task. For example, if you travel somewhere regularly on the bus or in the car, why not listen to something inspirational on the journey?

Aha, his mum was listening to motivational stuff in the car. He kept hearing the words pouring out of the car speakers, with little tips and nuggets of inspiration dropping into their Future Toolboxes.

In her part-time business, Milo noticed that his mum also hooked a habit of making a few calls whilst making a cup of tea. She would always say that she could make at least one call by the time the kettle boiled and would make another whilst she was drinking it.

Milo's Toolbox:
Take the thirty-day challenge and create a great new habit.
Use positive language and affirmations to enhance success.
Ask people for support and listen to them when they are helping you. Thank them for their input and make them feel valued that they are helping you achieve your goal.

Milo Challenges You:
Why not make a list of your bad habits? Be honest but don't beat yourself up if you have lots.

Take a look at your list and open your mind. Instead of just accepting that's the way you are, commit to change.

Try changing or creating one or two habits at a time.

If you fall off the wagon in your thirty days, dust yourself down and begin again. Remember failure only happens when you quit!

Fun Facts – Why do people do the things they do?
As an old saying goes, there is nothing as funny as folk (or nowt as funny as folk in the north of England)! Yep, us humans have the weirdest habits? Well there is no science behind the list below, they are just things we have observed people doing and will probably not admit to doing ourselves.

So why is it that when someone trips and stumbles in the street, they glare at the offending paving slab and they pretend they meant to do it?

How about checking your mobile phone seconds after the last time you checked it? What could have possibly happened in those few seconds? Some people even take it to the toilet with them. Or they put it on speaker phone and hold the phone vertically in front of their face to have a conversation. Why? There is an ear piece and a mouth piece. *Huffington Post* said that was annoying if the world can hear you too.

Ever noticed that when someone talks about time, they look at their wrist even though they aren't wearing a watch? In fact, they never wear watches at all. Why?

When you're sitting in a car at a red traffic light and the car next to you rolls forward a couple of centimetres. The car behind then rolls forward too... and then the one behind it. Yep, the lights are still on red and nobody is going anywhere.

Do you ever go to a coffee shop and end up people watching or pretend you are European by saying ciao and doing a continental kiss? Say like, basically, obviously, ermm or y'know excessively in conversations.

How do you dress yourself? Is it the same order… underwear, pants, shirt, socks, jacket maybe? Right sock on before left… you know you do.

Notice how people patting down their pocket to check for their wallet and keys even though they have just put them in there or they get their house keys out of their pocket or bag when they are three streets from home.

Perhaps you have a habit where, you read a list of habits and then question why everyone has these habits, even though you have those habits yourself but you will never admit to them.

G is for Goals – Turn Your Dreams into Realities

"I don't focus on what I'm up against. I focus on my goals and I try to ignore the rest." – Venus Williams (tennis champion)

It was Saturday and Milo wandered into the coffee shop ready to start his new job. Lois Latte greeted him and showed him how to work some of the machines and the till. He was now all ready to go.

"There you go, a cappuccino and an apple slice for you, sir, and a pot of tea and a scone for you, madam," he said, putting the order on the table in front of a couple who were his first customers of the day.

His first responsibilities were to take orders at the tables, take the drinks and snacks to the tables and then sort out their bills before taking payments.

"There's your change, hope you have a lovely day!"

"Thank you and good luck on your first day," came the reply from the tea-drinking lady, "and this is for you!" She popped a few coins onto the small tray containing the bill. It was Milo's first customer and his first tip. The day flew by, more customers and more tips. Ethan Espresso patted him on the back the back as he turned the door sign from open to closed.

"Well done Milo, you're a natural with the customers. They love you."

Ethan Espresso walked behind the counter and opened the tip jar, shook it for a few moments and looked up at Milo. He explained that Lois shared the tips between the staff at the end of the day and sure enough she did. He knew he wouldn't get paid until next week but Milo was delighted to finish his first day with cash in his hand. It felt like a real sense of achievement to have earned this money thanks to his friendly attitude to the customers and great service, it felt like a huge reward.

After running in the house and getting changed, it was off to the park to meet some friends for a kickabout. What better way to spend a sunny evening? After the game, they headed off to Father Russmuss's Food Box to hang out. When they got there, Rico asked Milo how his Future Toolbox journey was going.

A little surprised at Rico's interest, Milo fumbled out a few excited words about the session that he and a small group of students had had with their Future Toolbox Coaches that week. Fidelma, who was at the session, and a few others sat around a table and joined the conversation.

Milo recited the analogy he heard earlier; "Imagine a football match (it doesn't matter if you like football or not though), two teams are playing in a stadium in front of 90,000 spectators. The television cameras are broadcasting the match worldwide and the atmosphere is electric. The game is about to kick off and someone runs to each end of the pitch and removes both of the goal posts? It is impossible to score a goal now, what is going to happen to the match?"

"Well it is going to be a little boring," replied Molly from the group.

"Yeah that would be pointless as no one could win," replied Noah, "I would turn the TV off."

Milo then turned to the group and said, "That's right. It's the same as life. If we have nothing to aim at then life becomes… well a little boring and pointless! We can chat more if you want."

Some of the group broke into their own conversation but five of the friends, Milo, Fidelma, Rico, Molly and Noah carried on the chatter. Milo picked up his bag and took out his Future Toolbox book. He gave the others some paper and pens from an old notebook he had. As he tore the pages out, he said, "Wow, it isn't often a group of teens sit in a cafe and talk about life goals is it?"

Sensing an air of pride, he opened the book at the page G is for Goals and began reading.

"The one without dreams is the one without wings!" – Muhammad Ali (professional boxer, activist, and philanthropist)

According to studies by The Ford Foundation:
- One in five people have no idea what they want from life.
- Two thirds of people have an idea of what they want but have no plan of how to get it.
- One in ten people have specific well-defined goals but only half of them achieve them.
- The top 3% however, achieve their goals 89% of the time.

Do you want to be in the top 3%?

A whole series of books have been written on goal setting. There are thousands upon thousands out there but let's keep it really simple by asking the **Three Questions of Direction**:
1. Where are you now?
2. Where do you want to be?
3. How are you going to get there?

When we visit schools and ask students these questions, they usually reply with the following answers:
1. At school.
2. At home.
3. Walk or get lift/bus.

Great fun and obvious but we are going to look a bit deeper into these questions and work towards our **life goals**. Here we go…

1. Where are you now?
Skyscrapers are built on solid foundations so we are going to lay the foundations for our life.

Take a look at where you are now. Evaluate what you have achieved so far. Write down the strengths that you have. Make a list of your accomplishments and successes. Go on, write stuff down, small or big, last week or last year. It doesn't matter but **celebrate your successes** and build some positive thoughts.

By starting with a positive base, we have our solid foundations and we can move to the next stage.

2. Where do you want to be?
You can't hit a target that cannot be seen so we first need to set the goal.

Imagine that the world is your oyster.
We are going to remove all barriers from life and make it **impossible** to **fail**.

You need to imagine that you have the ability to do anything:

- What would you do if you knew you were guaranteed to succeed?
- What would you become?
- Where would you go?
- What would you own?

Be specific and realistic.
Now be honest, it has to be humanly possible. Please don't put down super powers or time travel. How cool would they be but they don't exist? Remember the planet we live on has its own rules. When it wants to rain it rains; we cannot change that. After autumn comes winter… we can't rearrange the seasons.

Also, it has to be legal of course.

At this stage, write down everything that springs into your mind and don't worry about how you will achieve these things yet. Again, remember Richard Branson's quote, *"If someone offers you an amazing opportunity and you're not sure you can do it, say yes – then learn how to do it later"* from **O is for Open Your Mind**? We'll think about the how later. You must also write down positive language of course. Instead of; "I don't want to be broke" write "I am financially free."

3. How are you going to get there?
Now we have a target in place, let's look at ways to achieve it.

The people who achieve their **goals** the most often are the ones who **have a plan** on how they are going to get what they want.

Specific **well-defined goals** have a better success rate so take your goal and look at it. Is it a big or small goal? If it's big then maybe you could break it down to smaller chunks. Perhaps it is a **massive goal** that is made up of a **number of smaller goals.**

A good way to do this is to work backwards. Look at the big picture first and ask what you need to achieve the top goal. Then what do you need to do in order to achieve the bit before and the bit before that, and so on.

Imagine you are preparing a fantastic dish for dinner and think of all the lovely ingredients that you put into it. Perhaps some of them need slicing, marinating or cooking first.

"A goal is a dream with a deadline" – Napoleon Hill (self-help author)

There is a difference between a dream or ambition and a goal and that is the **plan**. Here is a simple step-by-step process for building the foundations of your **goals**:

Step 1 – Turning the dream into a reality.
Take your list of dreams from the World is Your Oyster exercise and pick one goal. It may be a huge goal and there could be some smaller ones that that will help you achieve big.

Step 2 – Your why.
You why is huge! A goal without a why is going to lack foundation and if your why isn't big enough then you will have a lesser chance of achieving it. It's like a building built on sand without a foundation, it will fall down.

What is your why? Why are you really writing these things down? Do you really want these things or is it because the will impress someone else or because the someone else is telling you these things are good?

Your why has to be your why and not someone else's. These are your **goals**.

Make your why come from the heart, **feel the emotion** from it. You could even say that your why could make you cry because it is that powerful.

Step 3 – Timeline.
Set a date! Do you think you will achieve a goal by saying, "One day I might get around to learning to speak fluent Spanish?"

One day may never arrive! The chances of achieving this goal are slim because you are leaving it to chance. Don't take the risk.

Try saying, "By xxx date, I am speaking fluent Spanish!"

Now you have a deadline to work towards. This will help you to stay focussed.

Deadlines are amazing. Have you ever watched a sports match and seen a team who are losing suddenly step up their game with minutes left? They give it their all to score a point or a goal in order not to be defeated.

Do be realistic though, remember life will get in the way and there will be distractions. Please also note that a date will commit you but it can sometimes be moved if necessary.

Step 4 – What and how.
Now think of some basics you may need in order to achieve this goal.

Think of the steps you need to take. Perhaps this is where you need to break it down or even work backwards. You may have been asked the question, can you eat an elephant? You can indeed, one bite at a time. The first step might be to find out where elephants hang out before you even consider cutting into bite-sized chunks.

Break down your goal and think about what you need and how you will achieve it. Will it cost money and if so, how will you get the money? Do you need any **skills or qualifications** and where can you learn them from? Do you need any tools and if so, what?

Step 5 – Who.
Who is going to help, support and inspire you? Who could you study? Remember, the successful people have successful habits, study their habits and copy them. Borrow their enthusiasm and use them as a role model.

Sharing your goal with those people close to you can be a huge boost to help you achieving your **goals**.

189

Warning, warning, warning: some people may tell you that it is impossible or you can't or won't achieve your goals. Some people will be dream stealers who are probably jealous of your vision but some may be people who love you and want to protect your from failing.

Respect these people. Tell the loved ones that you value their opinion but tell them your why, it may help them to understand. As for the dream stealers, well… do it for you and not for them.

Step 6 – Be visual and focus.
A picture paints a thousand words, as the saying goes. Display a **picture of your goals** somewhere you can see it daily.

Actor Jim Carrey had a goal to make it in Hollywood. Aged nineteen, he was broke and pretty depressed with life but he jumped into a beat up and battered car and drove to the hills overlooking Los Angeles. There he pulled out a cheque book and wrote himself a cheque for $10 million and post-dated it ten years in the future. He popped it in his wallet where he could see it every day.

Amazingly ten years later, he was a multi-millionaire after starring in Hollywood movies including *Dumb and Dumber* and *Ace Ventura Pet Detective*.

The **laws of attraction** helped Jim achieve the goal by using this visual reminder. How about trying something similar yourself? Perhaps writing a mock certificate of achievement or superimposing yourself into a picture of you achieving your goal?

The food arrived as the group laughed with each other. Milo had a picture of a beach in SE Asia where he planned to spend New Year in two years' time. Fidelma, Noah, Molly and Rico all had their visions of success which included a house on top of a hill, a sleek sportscar, doing a parachute jump and playing lead guitar in a band on stage… yep the last one was Rico's.

Milo's Toolbox:
Set short and long-term goals.
Break the big goals down into smaller goals and work towards bite-sized chunks.
Use pictures and images to focus on to make sure the goal stays in the front of your mind.
Always state goals in positive language and visualise achieving them.
Remember, set goals in concrete but dates in sand, sometimes life can get in the way.

Milo Challenges You:
Follow a simple **goal** setting plan on a daily, weekly or monthly basis.

- Have a daily to do list and review at the end of the day. Aim to achieve 80% of the tasks on there.
- Perhaps use a journal to plan your day and review your goals on a weekly and monthly basis.
- Start by making a list of everything that you want to achieve and don't worry about how you will achieve it. The first step to success is having the **goal** in the first place.

Pick one **goal** and apply the above plan to it.

Fun Facts – Some goals can seem outrageous
Look into the sky and you will see a plane but when the Wright Brothers planned the first flight in 1903, the majority of people thought this was outrageous. They managed it and their goal has shaped world travel.

When Roger Bannister broke the four-minute mile barrier in 1954, so-called experts had said that it was impossible to run that fast but he proved to the world that he could achieve his goal.

You may well have heard about Martin Luther King who delivered his "I have a dream" speech and moved the world but goals don't always have to be as high profile as these mentioned. So, what are the most talked about goals that people put onto their bucket lists?

Extreme goals include bungee jumping, skydiving, cliff jumping, BASE jumping and storm chasing – be careful now. There's also the thrill of surfing, skiing, snowboarding, white-water rafting and kayaking.

Fancy a bit of travel? There are too many to mention but these are extremely popular and also quite a challenge; making it to both the North and South Poles, crossing a country or even a continent on a bike and circumnavigating the globe. Many people would like to trek the Inca Trail in Peru, climb to Everest Base Camp or walk the Great Wall of China.

Personal goals, again there are so many. What do people want to do for themselves? Learn a new language, achieve their ideal weight, run a marathon or take part in a triathlon. Helping others by being a mentor to someone or give to charity. Maybe starting a business, working from home, work for yourself or even publishing a book (yep, that was one of ours too).

Get your bucket list out and add to it. Why is it called a bucket list anyway? Ah well, it's believed to have come from the phrase, "to kick the bucket" which means to die. The bucket list therefore means "things to do before you die!" So where does kick the bucket come from? OK, too many questions now... let's move on.

F is for Failure – Fail Your Way to Success

"Many of life's failures are people who didn't realise how close they were to success when they gave up." – Thomas Edison (inventor and businessman)

Apart from being famous, what do all these people have in common?

- **Bill Gates, Albert Einstein** and **Stephen Spielberg**? They all dropped out of education at some point in their lives.
- How about **Steve Jobs** and **Walt Disney**? They were both fired from their jobs?

- Next up, **Abraham Lincoln, Stephen King** and **JK Rowling**? They all suffered great depression.
- Finally, **Michael Jordon, Jessie J, Colonel Sanders** and **Thomas Edison**? They were all rejected time and time again before finally making their name. In fact, all the above names suffered many knockbacks and failed over and over again.

Failure, is it really failing?
We have just used the word failed in the above sentence but failure really only means failure when you quit for good. To paraphrase Thomas Edison: **"Some people are so close when they decide to give up!"** Successful people will more than likely experience more knockbacks than any other people on this planet, simply because they keep going until they succeed.

Educational Failures.
Bill Gates dropped out of Harvard, plus co-owned a business that failed spectacularly before going on to become billionaire Microsoft creator.

Labelled "stupid" by his teachers, **Albert Einstein** struggled to speak even at the age of nine and later in life, was refused entry to Zurich Polytechnic school. He went on to win a Nobel Prize for physics in 1921.

Why was **Stephen Spielberg** rejected by the University of Southern California three times? Because of his poor high school grades, yet he went on to direct over fifty films.

These educational failures certainly overcame their barriers by showing that it is possible to succeed without qualifications. However, remember in **Q is for Quality**, it is better to put in the effort and give everything your best shot. A lesson from Spielberg, perhaps getting good grades would have helped him.

Fired.
Ironically, after setting up Apple, **Steve Jobs** was fired from the company. It turned out to be one of the best things to happen to him as it gave him a passion for success. Starting ventures including the

animation company Pixar, he ended up back at Apple as the Chief Executive Officer.

Walt Disney also dropped out of school and then was later fired from a newspaper company in Missouri for "not being creative enough". His venture Laugh-A-Gram Studios went bankrupt because his lack of business sense. Was he a failure? Bet you can name loads of Disney films, can't you?

Getting fired from a job or going bankrupt isn't a recommendation but it is how you respond to a knockback. Bingo… we talked about **R is for Response-Ability**. These guys certainly showed their **ability to respond** to a situation, didn't they?

Depression.
After also failing in business in, **Abraham Lincoln** suffered a nervous breakdown in 1836. This wasn't the end of him though, he went on to run for president in 1856 but was defeated in the election. He finally became president in 1861.

After a troubled childhood, **Stephen King** turned to drugs and alcohol in an attempt to battle depression. He later turned his emotions into writing and became the author we know today.

After her life imploded, **Joanne (JK) Rowling** went through divorce and became a single parent who was classed as poor. Living on state benefits and depressed she rose from rags to riches, selling over 400 million *Harry Potter* books. This is after being rejected by twelve publishers, some who thought her book was too long.

Rejected.
Everyone mentioned above has experienced many rejections but **Michael Jordon** was told he would never play basketball because he was "too short". **Jessie J** was thrown out of the school choir because her music teacher thought her voice was too good and showed up other students. This of course wouldn't have made her very popular and she was bullied for years. **Colonel Sanders** travelled across America approaching people to buy his fried chicken recipe and 1,009 people said

no. **Thomas Edison** was publicly told to quit trying to invent light bulbs after thousands of so-called failed experiments. He saw every experiment as a success because he had identified another way of how not to invent a light bulb.

Not one of these people became overnight success. Not one of them had an easy path, nor did they possess pots of money. Every one of them had their doubters, dream stealers and critics.

These are just a handful of people who we know as household names but what about the millions of other successful people who have gone on similar journeys? The wonderful trailblazers who raise money for charity, accomplish life changing events, save people's lives, give back to society, set up businesses in towns and cities all over the world, raise children and care for others? As mentioned in **Y is for Your Life**, it isn't just fame and fortune that measures success.

The above names are of famous people but many everyday people fail their way to success too. Milo recalled that his very own teacher Oli Switchblade failed his school exams. He told a story of how he ended up in a supermarket stacking shelves. Everyone around him including himself, saw him as a failure because university wasn't an option for him. However, he worked his way up to store manager and went on to study a part-time teaching qualification before moving into education.

Look at people around you? Have they always been a success?

We have a friend who dropped out of university in his twenties, actually leaving before he was kicked out. He went on to become a successful business owner, author and international public speaker without actually having a conventional job. This is just one of many friends we know who turned their failure into an opportunity for success.

We all make mistakes, get knockbacks, rejections, fall down, fail… whatever you want to call it… but remember, it is how we respond (**R is for Response-Ability**). Imagine if Thomas Edison had quit after a couple of light bulb experiments, the world would be a bit darker. If JK

Rowling decided to throw her book in the bin after the first rejection, millions of people wouldn't have enjoyed her stories and nobody would have heard of Harry Potter. If Steve Jobs or Bill Gates had thrown the towel in then we wouldn't be able to choose between Apple and Microsoft. Einstein wouldn't have shaped the world with his mathematical genius and try and imagine a world without Disney.

The world would be without many things that we take for granted if people hadn't taken the leap of faith and believed in themselves.

There are billions of ideas that we have never heard about because people have quit. There are millions of half-written novels and stories that people have never published, endless films that have never made the screens, countless things that have been invented but never used, songs written but never sung... legacies never created all because a particular person quit.

OK, you may not be a world-changing pioneer... or maybe you will. Someone has to be, why not you? It is time to focus on your world, what will be your purpose? What are those goals you set in **G is for Goals**? What will you achieve? What is your purpose?

Dealing with rejection.
You will fail, experience knockbacks and feel rejection, and rejection is probably the hardest of all to take. This is where you have to stay focussed on your end goal and keep visualising what it will feel like when you have achieved it.

Not only are we our own biggest critics at times but the comments of others are the ones that hit us hard and hurt the most.
- "I'm sorry Mr Sanders but your fried chicken isn't going to work in our restaurant!"
- "Dear Mrs Rowling, thank you for submitting your story about the wizard boy but it is too long and won't fit into our plans at this stage!"
- "Albert, please leave our school, you are clearly not intelligent enough and you will never amount to anything!"

- "Dear you, thank you for attending the interview for your dream job but you have been unsuccessful on this occasion!"
- Your name + your grade = 🙁
- "I know you are starting your own business but I won't be supporting you, I am going elsewhere!"

You will hear these things throughout your life… in fact, you've already heard thousands of these statements already, haven't you?

"What if I fail though?"
Remember the **Future Toolbox** phrase, **it's acceptable to try really hard and to not succeed but it is not acceptable to not try and still fail.**

So, what next?
Do you quit or do you **come back stronger**? Your **ability to respond** is key!

Visualise how you will feel when you have achieved your goal. Repeat, repeat – visualise how you will feel when you have **achieved your goal**. Focus, focus… I am going to the top of my mountain whether you like it or not Mr Rejection, Mrs Doubter, Sir Knockback, Madam Failure… I don't care what you think. This is my journey so I am asking you to politely step aside.

Failure is temporary, but quitting is permanent.

Milo popped down his book. He failed a few of his exams in school and there seemed a lot of pressure on him to pass these from his parents and teachers. How did he respond? Some subjects he stopped trying in and engaging in class because he didn't see the point. He quit music because he could never master playing an instrument. On the other hand, he was so far behind on his maths coursework but spent extra time with his maths teacher to catch up and get back on track for his grade. It wasn't his number one choice, his mum found out at parents' evening and suggested that this would be a good idea. The teacher agreed and there was no way of avoiding maths for an extra two hours a week after school.

He finished last in one of first cross-country events because the field was good but he decided to keep training because he enjoyed it.

Milo's Toolbox:
Failure isn't failure unless I quit altogether.
Stay focussed on my goals and expect knockbacks and critics.
Try to encourage others to achieve their goals, don't be the person who steals their dreams.

Milo Challenges You:
Make a list of things that you have quit because you have failed.
Pick a goal that you could pick back up and achieve if you really worked at it.
Go back to **G is for Goals** and follow the goal-setting steps.

Later we are going to look at how to change our mindsets and work towards achieving them.

Fun Facts – Is this a failure or a pretty good effort?
Anyone who has taken a driving test and failed isn't alone, it is reported that over 830,000 tests are failed every year. There is actually a rumour that a South Korean woman failed her driving test over 771 times. Would you get in the car with this driver?

However, here are some really bizarre world record attempts that failed to make the grade:
- It took a whole month for a Dutch team to set up four million dominoes for a world record attempt to topple them all. Oh no, a sparrow got trapped in a building and knocked a lot of them

down before the day of the attempt and they decided to abandon ship.

- In Iran, over 1,000 cooks attempted to make the world's longest sandwich in 2008. Trouble is, the large crowd were too impatient to wait for the main dish and started eating the 1,500-metre-long sandwich before it had been officially measured. A great effort all the same.

- Never play with fire. Well these people probably shouldn't! In New Zealand, a group tried to set a new world record for fire-walking in 2004. Unfortunately, the wrong type of wood was used and twenty-eight people ended up in hospital suffering from burns. They decided to quit and accept failure on this one.

- As we know, people try the weirdest things but sometimes they fail before they have even begun. The world record attempt for the most people inside a bubble at one time also failed at the last minute in California, 2012. Everything was set to go but a local TV reporter managed to break the bubble machine and ruined the attempt.

- You have to feel for thrill seeking French adventurer Michel Fournier who, in 2008, was about to attempt to break the sound barrier by skydiving from a balloon from thirty-four kilometres (twenty-one miles) above the earth's surface. He was about to board the balloon for his journey into the sky but it detached itself from its capsule whilst being inflated and floated away into the heavens. All he could do is watch in horror.

E is for Exercise – Look After Your Body

"Those who think they have not time for bodily exercise will sooner or later have to find time for illness." – Edward Stanley (Nineteenth century Prime Minister, Fourteenth Earl of Derby)

Lungs busting, sweat pouring, Milo dug with his legs screaming as he pushed up the short hill. "Whose idea was it to run this far?" he muttered as a fellow runner drew alongside him in The Fantastic Funtopia 5K. This was Milo's first ever running event that he had taken part in outside of the school cross country. His dad was somewhere in the field too and Milo took some satisfaction knowing he was behind him as a bit of family competition had been bandied around the house in the week leading up to the event.

Reaching the top of the hill, he looked up and saw the finish line in sight. There was a small crowd of people, including Thea and their mum, cheering the runners home. Milo kept his focus ahead and attempted to speed up a little to get to the end a little quicker. The noise of the crowd got a little louder as he made the final strides over the line before slowing to a stop and putting his hands on his knees. Whilst battling to get his breath back, a hand landed on his shoulder and he heard the words, "Hey man, that was awesome!" The voice was familiar, it was Ice Man Isaac, one of the best runners in the school cross country team, "You nailed it buddy, that was a strong finish. I'm super proud of you, man!"

Isaac had a habit of always being positive and over-using friendly phrases like man, mate, buddy as well as upbeat words like super, awesome and amazing. Milo had been a little intimidated by how successful he was when he first joined the team because Isaac seemed to make everything look easy and his confidence was always 100%. Even studying seemed effortless, he was used to getting top grades and nothing seemed to stress him out. Because of his cool, calm approach to everything, he got the nickname Ice Man Isaac.

They had never really spoken before but when Milo went to his first training session, Isaac came over and shook his hand and welcomed him. Milo was taken back as his didn't think Isaac even knew who he was but the support from the top boy in the team was brilliant.

"Yeah, your training paid off there, bud, it shows that if you keep working hard then you will be amazing!"

Sweat was now dripping onto the floor from his head and his heart rate was bouncing but Milo managed a thumbs up.

"Anyway, you get your breath back and I'll come back and big you up even more, you superstar," he concluded handing him a bottle of water.

This meant a lot to Milo to receive so much praise from someone who was top of his game. Anyway, where's Dad he thought to himself. He saw him coming along the finish straight. Standing up and trying to steady himself, Milo thought it would be best to make it look as if the race had been easy when his dad crossed the line, there was a lot of family pride at stake here.

"Wow, well done, Dad," he congratulated him, handing him his water bottle.

"Man, that was the hardest thing I've ever done in my life," came the reply between deep breaths and the occasion curse. Milo knew it was only words of pain in the moment. "Anyway, you don't look like you've even broken a sweat!"

Milo circled his shoulders backwards and nodded his head with a smirk on his face.

"Yeah, y'know, it was a breeze," he bragged pretending he was like Ice Man Isaac now. Truth is, he felt exactly the same only moments ago but it was time to play down his achievement as Thea and mum rushed over to join in the praise.

Back home, they both grabbed a snack and dad collapsed onto the sofa, still wearing his running kit. Milo decided it was time for some reading.

"Take care of your body. It's the only place you have to live." – Jim Rohn (entrepreneur, author and motivational speaker)

You can't throw away your body and buy a new one or change parts on it. You can however improve it with two components to a **healthy lifestyle – diet and exercise**. We have already talked about food in **V is for Vegetables** so let's have a look at the exercise part.

The hardest step to exercise for most people is the first step out of the door and having the willpower to commit.

Go to any town or city in the world and you are spoilt for choice with gyms to join. The gym analogy is a perfect example. *Which?* magazine reported that Brits waste £37 million pounds a year on unused gym memberships. Yep that's right, if you join a gym, you do actually have to go to it to make it work. This is where millions of people fail to get out of the front door because perhaps the lure of the TV or sofa is more appealing.

The world is full of so much convenience too, this means that less effort is required to get somewhere. For example, a friend of mine lives less than a mile from work but still jumps in his car to get to work, even on glorious sunny days. The truth is, it would actually be a lot quicker to walk by the time he has sat in traffic, found a parking space and then walked the final steps into the office.

OK, perhaps the gym isn't for you or you have no desire to run a race? Well there are numerous inexpensive or even free, and less strenuous activities that you can take part in to keep fit and active. Our car-driving friend here could make a simple walk of a mile and a half daily to and from work and get greater health benefits surely? It really is that simple.

So how do we get started? Let's use the **G is for Goals** setting process here.

Where are you now with your fitness?
Perhaps you are quite fit and want to improve. Maybe you find it hard to walk up the stairs without being out of breath. You could be slightly over your ideal weight. Keep this bit simple and don't over-complicate it.

Where do you want to be with your fitness?
Maybe you want ensure you stay active. Perhaps you want to be able to climb the stairs and feel great at the top. You may want to lose a little weight. Perhaps you *do* want to run a race or build muscle at the gym.

How are we going to get there and achieve our fitness goals? Well remember that not all **fitness** has to be high intensity or extreme like climbing a mountain or lifting heavy weights. Perhaps it could be walking around the block or the park every day, maybe taking a walk or cycling instead of taking the car or bus.

Remember to be realistic too, it is much harder to commit to joining a sports club, walking group, gym or cycling club that is based an hour from your home. Find something close by to make it easier to get out of the door on a cold, dark and wet evening.

The next key point may sound obvious but pick something that you are going to enjoy and appreciate. It is pointless buying a judo outfit if you don't like martial arts. Also, remember that you don't have to compete at things if you don't want to. Friendly competition can help but some people just like to simply take part and that is OK.

Ding-dong. The message tone sounded on Milo's phone with a text giving him his result of his run earlier. Excitedly he picked up his mobile and it slipped out of his hands onto the floor. As he bent down to pick it up, he heard another text message tone come from the other room on his dad's mobile.

"Yesss," his dad called in triumph, "A minute quicker than I expected," he said, sitting up from his slouched sofa position and punching his fist above his head.

"Us pros remembered to start our watch though," Milo smugly pointed out as he fired a text to Isaac to let him know of his progress and victory over his dad. Isaac was almost two minutes ahead of Milo though but he had pointed out that he had a benchmark to beat if he wanted to.

The father-son banter continued as they continued to vow to beat each other at the next event. His dad made a few excuses that Milo had got lucky or that the weather wasn't quite right. It was all good fun though. As his dad hobbled out of the room, Milo called out, "Old man," and picked up his journal and noted:

- Event date and time.
- Target time.
- Did I enjoy the event? Yes.
- Is this going to benefit me health wise? Yes.
- Can I do it? Of course.
- How often do I want to train? Two to three times a week.
- Who can help me? Isaac and the will to keep beating my dad.

The goal is set, train two to three times a week with the cross-county guys and his dad to achieve his goal time. Time to pull out his planner and put in his training sessions.

"You've got no chance of beating me... ever haha," he yelled out to his dad.

"I'm coming for you, Son," came the reply.

"If you are in a bad mood go for a walk. If you are still in a bad mood go for another walk." – Hippocrates (ancient Greek physician)

Back to you. So, what is your goal?
- Maybe walking around the block five times a week. Walking at a steady pace has so many incredible health benefits.
- Walk to school/college/work instead of taking the bus/driving/getting a lift. If it's too far, how about getting off the bus a stop earlier or parking the car a little further away from your destination?
- If you fancy something a little more intense, maybe run for ten seconds and walk for ten and increase this. Do five press ups, rest and do five more (Oli Switchblade style). Lift a 1 kg weight and gradually increase it to 2 kg weights.
- A good friend of ours ran a marathon recently. Her first experience was joining a beginners' running group and starting a training plan of lap of the park, running for thirty seconds and walking for thirty seconds. She ran the whole 26.2 miles.

Keep It Up.

Like any success goals, consistent effort is required. Sometimes it will hurt, sometimes a better offer will come up – life gets in the way. If you miss a session, pick up the plan and get back on track. Focus on the goal and enjoy the journey.

Warning, warning.

Take care not to celebrate all of your hard work when you reach your goal by over indulging. For example, you could reach your target weight and then start eating all the wrong foods again. That would be a shame. You could complete the event that you have been training hard for and then stop doing the activity. Why not enter another event? You could just become busy with all those life things and then find yourself saying how much you miss it. Let's get started again.

Why do nothing when you can do something?

Have you ever noticed that when you do nothing then nothing happens? Yet too many people sit around and wait for things to happen. They leave their fate to chance and the chances are… it won't happen. **Proactive people** are the ones who more forward and achieve more. The ones who blame their circumstances do not. How many times do we say that we can't be bothered? And guess what, time still passes and someone else will be bothered.

Milo's Toolbox:

I am fit and active now but I intend to stay that way.

Join a club, having others working towards fitness goals will help me achieve mine. Be inspired by others who are good at what I do and learn from them. Like-minded people will support each other.

207

Balance my fitness and healthy eating to ensure I look after my body.

Milo Challenges You:
As the **Future Toolbox** says, set your **fitness** goals. There is not one size fits all approach but think of something that you enjoy doing and perhaps want to try.

Remember, you may think you are "rubbish" at first, but **practice makes progress.**

If there is a training plan then follow it but make sure it is realistic to fit into your life and your capabilities too. Beware that people can become obsessed with weight loss, exercise or trying to look like something and the obsession will lead to either neglect of something else or no longer enjoying the routine. Make sure you keep enjoying what you do.

Fun Facts – Exercise is great but is this too much?
It's great to exercise with a group of people to get a bit of moral support but in India the world's largest yoga lesson was held, an incredible 35,985 people took part. Now where's my yoga mat?

Think you will get too old to exercise? Well, Canadian Ida Herbert who was an active fitness instructor at the age of ninety-five years old in 2012.

Mao Weidong from China gained the record for the longest time holding an abdominal plank position in eight hours and one minute in 2016. Now that's abs of steel.

All sound a bit serious, how about a piggy back race? A bit of fun and a good workout too. In 2012, Australia 710 scouts and friends completed the biggest ever piggy back race in history.

Weight lifting is good too but in 2013 Steve Schmidt lifted a 100 kg weight sixty times in one minute using only his teeth. Seriously, use your arms in future.

Finally, people love the treadmill in the gym but Tony Mangan of Ireland clocked up a forty-eight-hour stint on a treadmill, covering over 250 miles which was a record at the time. It was soon beaten but then Mangan beat it again and… will you just stop now.

D is for Desires – Needs versus Wants

"Too many people spend money they haven't earned to buy things they don't want to impress people they don't like." – Will Rogers (Twentieth-century actor)

"Good morning everyone, my name is Carol Cashier from Moola Bank. It is a pleasure to be here with you all on this lovely Tuesday morning to talk about money."

It was a totally optional session at school today but Milo, Rico and a few other friends went along to learn about money.

"This time next year I'm gonna be a millionaire," Rico belted out before grinning and looking around the room to see who he had impressed. Carol Cashier stopped in her tracks and looked a little unimpressed but continued to talk about the simple facts of bank accounts, interest, investments and taxes.

After the failure of his last joke, Rico tried again. "Taxes... taxi for Milo..." whilst pushing him in the arm. Carol again raised her eyebrows to state a look of "really?" at him. "Milo is loaded you know, he's working at the local coffee shop. He's gonna look after his mates, I'm getting a Ferrari!" Carol paused again and then continued talking and Milo shot a glare at his mate as he wanted to hear what she was going to say next.

Thinking about the tips he received from Lois Latte at the weekend and how he would get paid his salary soon too, he would have more money than ever before and will have earnt every single penny of it. New trainers, a computer game, that top he'd seen in the clothes shop window, a trip to the cinema and perhaps some food afterwards. The spending list had already begun in his head. In fact, some was spent at Father Russmuss's Food Box on Saturday evening.

I want, I want, I want...

Ever notice how young kids are great at telling everyone what they want? I want an ice cream, I want to go to the park, I want my mummy/daddy.

As we become teens and adults our wants change. We want the latest technology gadget, a fast food snack, a cool car, a new item of the latest fashion or a bigger house. But how much do we really need it?

Some people are victims of the powerful media and advertising that is in our faces each and every day. Some of us are drawn in to the clever marketing departments of these multi-million pound organisations.

Weigh up the benefits before you make the purchase. Ask yourself if you really need it.

Mobile phone companies tell us we need the latest smartphone. The new one is thinner and lighter but is it worth an extra £500? Yes, £500 and some cost more than that. Well, a lot of people think they're free but we'll find out how that works later.

Fast-food companies tell you how lovely their new, low fat (high sugar, processed carb loaded) meal tastes and it never quite looks the same as the picture. Is it worth that five minute binge that will leave you feeling hungry within the hour?

Car companies tell us to buy the latest eco-fuel saving car that will save lots of money at the petrol pump (but will cost tens of thousands to buy). Isn't it funny that all the adverts show the car driving through a city with no traffic, where does that exist?

Buy these football boots and you will play like your hero. This item of clothing will make you look like this celebrity. Make up, haircare or skincare that makes you look "perfect". Even washing powder adverts haven't changed much over the years, the "new improved" brand claims to be better than the old one.

It is tempting to buy and easy to pay for on our contactless cards or smartphone apps now, but do you really "need" it?

The **impulse zone** in your brain is fantastic but use it wisely. Firstly, you need to bring the impulse zone back to the sensible and sometimes boring, reality safety zone.

Of course, it is good to own nice things and enjoy them but think about the following points before you splash out:

Instant gratification...
- Will your spend make you feel better in the short term or will it benefit you in the future?
- List as many worthwhile benefits of owning this item as you can.
- Is your spend a priority? Do you have that amount of money? If so, should it be spent elsewhere first (for example, paying a bill

or clearing a debt)? Will it add financial pressure if you spend the money (now or on credit)?

- If you are buying on credit, can you afford the monthly payment over the agreed time? How much interest is being added on? Do you want to be paying for the item for that long?

Remember, new-item novelty wears off quickly. Many people get bored of things very soon and either don't use them and put them in a cupboard or sell them for much less. Amazingly when we talk to teens about money, they sometimes feel that they will be able to sell things for much more than they bought them for. This is unrealistic of course. Have a look around your house and note items that you don't use any more and think about how much they cost and how much value you or your household got from them.

Finally, if you can justify buying the item then great but shop around, could you get a better deal somewhere else?

Must-have mobile phone mentality.
This doesn't just apply to mobile phones but here is a good analogy of how many people buy in the impulse zone. We love our gadgets and nothing tops the "must have" list more than a shiny new mobile phone. One of the girls in the group called Katy recently saw an advert to "upgrade to the latest handset" in a shop on the high street. Her current phone has a few scratches on it but it works great. It does everything she needs it to but the offer is too good not to look at.

The advert says the handset has no up-front cost. Great, a free phone she thinks. The contract is for twenty-four months (two years) and will cost her £55 per month including free unlimited texts, calls and data.

Should she splash out and treat herself? Imagine opening the box, removing the phone from the packaging, peeling off the plastic protective covering and unravelling the wires for the first time.

Stop right there! Let's move from the impulse zone to the sensible and sometimes boring, reality **safety zone** and look at some practical (and boring facts) before we make our decision and sign a contract.

Firstly, the cost. Let's assume the cost for the sim package (or call bundle part) is £20 per month. This means the handset is £35 per month. No upfront cost doesn't mean the phone is free, it means that you will pay for it over a period of time. Here's the maths:

Handset £35 x 24 months = £840
Sim £20 x 24 = £480
Total cost over the next two years would be £1,320

Is that shiny new mobile phone really worth over £800? Ask yourself those questions you began with. Will the novelty last for two years? How exciting was your last mobile phone when you first got it and is it still as exciting now? If yes, why are you considering buying a new one? Finally, remember, in **W is for Wonga**, we talked about assets and liabilities. The mobile phone is a liability (in financial cost as well as time) and will depreciate in value.

The final question: Do you really **NEED** it?

This is a typical example of an instant gratification or impulse buy. Yes, sometimes we should treat ourselves but remember to have a healthy respect for money and become financially literate. Sadly, money isn't taught in school, there are no exams on wealth so it is up to us as individuals of all ages to study it and understand basic budgeting and economics.

I was lucky enough to be brought up by a family of careful spenders. "Look after the pennies and the pounds will look after themselves," was a regular saying when pocket money was issued. My mum, a book-keeper, educated me that if I wanted something then I should save up for it. She also taught me if I needed something, then I should also save for it.

Carol Cashier continued, "At eighteen years old, your mailbox, whether it be post, email, text, mobile phone, social media feed and so on, will be flooded with clever messages of products and goods usually financed by credit. Buy now, pay later, loans or credit card offers will be thrown into your face from every angle as

these seemingly caring organisations will welcome you to spend, spend, spend. Your spending and internet surfing habits are tracked by advertising agencies to cleverly drop adverts and promotions in front of you to target your impulse zone. Have a look at your internet screen on a computer and you will notice a pattern right in front of you.

"Beware though, as tempting as the offer may be, remember needs versus wants. People of all ages are targeted by retailers to spend their money with them and encouraged to think in the impulse zone.

"This applies to any purchase especially those where you can pay over a period of time. The example above could be on interest free credit which means the cost is divided by the number of months the agreement is for.

"Also, some credit agreements will charge extra interest. For something priced at £840, even with interest charged at 5%, you would pay just over an extra £40."

The impulse zone sounds exciting. A place where danger can occur for the daring. It can be the make-or-break zone and sometimes a good place to act when making decisions. It can also be the opposite though. We know the risks when someone makes a decision to take a substance, drive a car when over the limit, hit someone after an argument or do something else they may regret. Financial decisions are no exception.

The group left the session and Milo went over to Carol Cashier and politely thanked her for her advice.

"You are very welcome indeed, if I can help you a little then I know I have done my job today. You are more than welcome to come to our bank and open a savings account for some of your money that your friend was talking about earlier. We like to look after millionaires," she joked whilst glancing at Rico who was closing in behind him.

"Cheers Carol, top one," said Rico cheekily, "I need to be a millionaire!" He wandered out of the door rubbing two fingers on his thumb to indicate he had lots of money.

"Ah sorry about him," Milo said as he shook Carol's hand and left the room with a savings account leaflet.

"No worries at all."

"I've realised that I don't need that new mobile phone now," Katy said. "Thank you Carol, you've just saved me lots of money. I'll stick with my current phone for now!"

Milo began thinking about the message and how what he was going to do with his first salary and tips from the coffee shop. He wanted a new pair of trainers, the computer game, that top he'd seen in the clothes shop window, a trip to the cinema and perhaps some food afterwards but did he need them? He had two pairs of trainers so they were crossed off the list immediately. The top, hmm, don't need that. Computer game, a definite luxury and the cinema trip and food are entertainment. He does want all of those things but decided to have one treat as he had worked hard. The cinema it would be.

Milo's Toolbox:
Make my list of things I want to buy.
I am allowed to treat myself but I would like to save some money too so I'll make an appointment at the bank and start right away. Put together a budget plan, start saving but look at essential spending as well.

Money Terms to Understand.
Income Tax and National Insurance – we have to pay them whether we agree with them or not.

Residual, passive or royalty income – where you get paid for something over and over again for a piece of work. Musicians release a song and then are paid royalties every time their song is played or sold.

Equity is the difference between a loan amount and the value of something, such as your mortgage (a loan to buy a house) and the value of your house. For example, if your mortgage is £100,000 and your house is valued at £150,000 then you have £50,000 equity. This equity will be tied into your house and the only way to release it is to sell the house or take out another loan.

Milo Challenges You:
Everyone's financial situation is different so there isn't a one size fits all approach. For example, if you're a teen in school, you're not yet old enough to have credit cards, loans or mortgages. However, start by creating a **money mindset**. Spending more money than you earn is route one to disaster. Think about the spending tracker in from **W is for Wonga**. If you have a weekly allowance, do you save any of it? Do you borrow money from your friends? If so, that is now a debt. There is a great book called, *Rich Dad Poor Dad for Teens* by Robert Kiyosaki, we recommend you read it and add plenty more financial wisdom to your **Future Toolbox.**

For adults, list your weekly/monthly outgoings one by one. Are there any amounts that you could do without? For example, millions of adults pay for extended warranty insurance for products they no longer own, they pay gym memberships for gyms they don't attend and pay expensive credit agreements when they could get a lower rate.

Fun facts – Do you need or want all this weird stuff?

Sometimes you just can't help your impulsive instinct and you just have to buy something but for some people, it is just an addiction. Here are some people who have the biggest and weirdest collections in the world:

- Take Manfred Rothstein from North Carolina who owns 675 back scratchers, does he need to scratch that itch that many times?

- We have mentioned the desire to upgrade our mobile phones already but Carsten Tews from Germany has a collection of over 1,500 different mobile phones.

- She will certainly never smell, Carol Vaughan, from Birmingham, owns more than 1,300 bars of soap but that's not as weird as a guy called Rob Hull who has collected over 1,800 daleks. Surely *Doctor Who* won't be visiting him in a hurry.

- It gets even more off the scale when you take these: American Nancy Hoffman has 730 umbrella sleeves and Paul Brockman, from California, has a collection of over 55,000 dresses that he claims are all for his wife. Jackie Miley's teddy bear collection consists of over 8,000 bears but Deb Hoffmann is *Winnie the Pooh* mad and has over 14,000 Pooh-related items. Fancy a water fight? Chris Reid will beat you as he has over 240 super soakers. If you make a mistake, Petra Engels owns 19,571 erasers and if that makes you feel a little queasy, Dutch collector Niek Vermeulen has 6,290 airsick bags. If you need to clean your teeth, Grigori Fleicher from Russia has 1,320 toothbrushes and Martina Schellenberg from Germany owns more than 125,850 napkins, you can wipe your mouth afterwards. Finally, Hawaiian Donald Dettloff owns around 650 different surfboards – hang ten!

C is for Compound Effect – The Little Things

"Small, Smart Choices + Consistency + Time = Radical Difference."
– Darren Hardy (American author and former publisher of *SUCCESS* magazine)

Wednesday lunchtime chatter around the table was normally littered with opinions and today was no different. A mix of girls and boys talked about the latest TV show, two girls were swapping recommendations on their latest favourite music and a few others were talking sport.

Feeling a little reflective today, Milo was sitting quietly listening to the mixture of words coming from so many mouths. There was a constant battle between everyone to be heard and interruptions into each other's sentences. He was picking a moment to perhaps join a conversation. "These people need to read L is for Listen," he thought to himself.

Suddenly there was a pat on his back which almost caused him to spit his food out. In the moment of shock, he spun his neck around to confront whoever it was that disturbed his quiet moment but he noticed that it was Mr Switchblade standing over him.

"Press ups," he shouted whilst flexing his muscles, "I'm up to sixty a day now!" He mimicked a champion celebrating by raising both arms in the air, flexed his muscles again and wandered off triumphantly. Milo chuckled as his tutor looked silly in his gesture.

"Have you got a six-pack?" came a smart comment from Ice Man Isaac. Mr Switchblade turned and jabbed his knuckles into his body between his stomach and chest before pulling another muscle pose, spinning around on his heel and continuing his journey.

The bell sounded and it was time to leave. Milo crammed the last bit of his food into his mouth and realised he had missed out on the chance to talk music, sport or TV. Oh well, it was time to register and then a free period in the library followed where students got a chance to catch up on study. When he arrived, he emptied his bag, arranged his work on the table and popped his journal down next to his notebooks. He and the other students following the Future Toolbox Programme had been invited to produce a piece of work as part of their coursework which would count to their final grade and he jumped at the chance because it is always good to work on something enjoyable. He flipped open his book and started to read the next chapter.

The small, seemingly insignificant, moment to moment choices add up to the big results.

Everything in the book so far has been about the **compound effect**. It is the little things you do consistently every day shape that your future. So how does that work?

Let's imagine that you were to go to your favourite fast food takeaway and eat there every single day for ten years, what would happen? When we ask school students in **Future Toolbox** sessions, they usually reply that you would get fat, be ill or die. Sounds dramatic but you would be eating processed fats, sugars and empty carbohydrates and more than likely develop poor eating habits, gain weight, your complexion would change and the risk of heart disease or other illnesses like diabetes would increase. You can actually die from those diseases so perhaps it doesn't sound that dramatic after all.

Now if you were to visit your favourite fast food takeaway and eat there now, what would happen to you today?

"Erm, not much!"
That's right, the answer would be, "absolutely nothing!" OK you may feel slightly full, satisfied or even hungry for another but fundamentally nothing would happen long term. You wouldn't gain any weight, break out in spots or suffer a heart attack. If that was the case, chances are you wouldn't eat one, would you?

A small choice once, today, would make no noticeable difference but that small choice repeated time and time again would add up to a huge result.

"Hands up if you are sometimes late for school, even just a couple of minutes!"

Let's presume that you are only two minutes late for school – would you fail your exams?

"Of course not!"

OK, the average school has five lessons a day (some have six but we'll say five for now).

Imagine you are two minutes late for each lesson – 2 x 5 = 10 minutes.

If you were to miss ten minutes of study, would you fail your exams?

"No, of course I wouldn't!"

Well you spend five days a week at school so 5 x 10 minutes is now fifty minutes, let us round it up to one hour for ease. Would you fail your exams for missing an hour of study?

"No way, I wouldn't!"

Most students attend school for around thirty-eight weeks a year so 38 x 1 hour now equals thirty-eight hours.

Most school lessons are more or less an hour long so the question is, "If you were to miss more than thirty-eight lessons in school, do you think this may start affecting your exam results?"

The answer now is, perhaps it would! This isn't necessarily just about the time though, it is also about the knock-on effects too. Your teacher is annoyed because of your bad habit of always being late so they tell you off. You react and blame the bus that makes you late every day. The teacher tells you to get an earlier bus but the truth hurts so you answer back again and perhaps end up getting detention. How is your mood now? Do you feel like learning? Even if you didn't it is unlikely that you are going to give that lesson your 100% attention. Two minutes has now become a whole lesson of less-effective learning. Is this going to affect your exams now? Erm, yes!

"So how can I make a positive approach to the compound effect?"

It's not just teens here, adults sometimes have these poor habits at work or in life in general, so the first step is **H is for Habits** – create a new and positive habit. Is it easy to be two minutes early instead of two minutes late? Of course, it is and that's a start.

If you were to eat a healthy snack instead of a sugary or processed fatty one pretty much every day then you would be leaner, fitter and healthier. That is the **compound effect**.

If you chose to study extra for fifteen minutes a day instead of watching TV, going on social media or playing computer games then you would learn more. Yep, **compound effect** again. Here's some more ideas...

Instead of reading a newspaper full of negative stories and opinions, read ten pages of a motivational book instead. Perhaps even turn off the radio and replace it with a motivational CD to listen to, or watch an inspirational online video from someone successful and inspirational instead of a cat falling off a table or a dog running into a window. If you were walking instead of driving, taking the bus or getting a lift then you would be more active and therefore be fitter.

- Take the stairs instead of the escalator or lift.
- Ask a question instead of moaning that you don't know the answer.
- Smile instead of frown.
- Praise instead of criticise.
- A good deed instead of a selfish task. Be kind.
- Take a pause after hearing something instead of immediately reacting.
- Save a penny instead of disregarding it... the list goes on and, as you are aware, many of these little habits have been mentioned many times in previous chapters and put into your **Future Toolbox.**

The small and sometimes seemingly insignificant, boring things you do daily will add to the big results.

Think of some ideas of things that you could change easily. Things that may only take moments of our day and they are easy to do. There is a catch though, things that are easy to do are also easy not to do. As you won't see any significant, instant result, it is easy to dismiss them or forget them altogether.

One idea could be to set a daily reminder in your phone to act on your **compound effect**? That will remind you to make your simple steps in the right direction.

"I trained for seventeen years and 114 days to become an overnight success." – Lionel Messi (professional footballer)

Some people think that one day it will all happen. One day a magic wand will make their dreams come true but it will be the moment to moment choices made up until that day that will create the result. Lionel Messi's quote proves this fact. We all see a superstar appear in the limelight of fame and heard about the big, lucky break they had when they "made it" but in reality, we don't see the years and years of hard work, slogging, failures and rejections they have experienced. Go back and read about the famous failures in **F is for Failure**.

On 20th July 1969, the world watched as Neil Armstrong stepped from Apollo 11 and said, "That's one small step for a man, one giant leap for mankind." As he set foot on the moon's surface, everyone saw that small single action but what they didn't see was the years of planning that went into it. President John F. Kennedy publicly set the goal in 1961. The Apollo program took a further eight years to achieve and was estimated that over 400,000 engineers, technicians, and scientists worked on the programmes which cost $24 billion (close to $100 billion in today's dollars).

The idea of studying is the same. Why do you think everyone spends so many years at school, college or university and then sit a final exam at the end? You cannot expect to miss the whole academic year, cram everything the night before the exam and pass with flying colours. It's the little choices to study and learn that will equal success.

A career is the same, nobody gets promoted on day one, it takes years of experience. Businesses don't become successful overnight but it will be built on every little decision made, every piece of effort given and all the sweat and stress spent making it work. Athletes train and train and train and train. They go through the same boring sessions, the same pains and the same routines to become a winner. Most of the time though, we don't notice these processes and habits, we just see the end result.

After all, **practice makes progression** and all these small habits and practices will positively compound over time.

"To try or not to try, that is the question..."
Shakespeare famously said that didn't he? OK, it wasn't quite that but success requires effort and sometimes effort or trying is hard work and boring.

Plant – cultivate – harvest.
A successful farmer will **plant** their crop, **cultivate** it by watering it, caring for it, keeping the weeds away, protecting it from insects and birds eating it and finally he will **harvest** it when it's ready. Sometimes we miss out the cultivate and expect things to happen without effort. The **compound effect** is all about the cultivating, you can't expect plant then harvest to work.

Every day we make hundreds of decisions, mostly without really thinking. If you can pause for a moment and think if this a habit that you have been following for a long time and decide if it is a good or not so good one. If it isn't good, perhaps it is time to change, create a new one and think of the positive effect it will have long term.

In the future, there will be no firework display, Mardi Gras or fanfare of music, you will be based on a sum total of all those simple actions over time.

From that moment of realisation, it becomes a case that every single moment of your life can be as important as the next.

Milo sat up in his chair, changing his position for a moment. He opened his eyes a little wider and put his hand on the side of his face. Thinking back to lunchtime and Switchblade's cameo role in the dinner hall announcing his progress on the press up challenge. Only weeks ago, his teacher said he couldn't do a single press up, yet now he was doing over sixty in a day and working up to 100.

His dad's fitness plan was going well by adding a little extra distance and a few minutes each time and now he managed a 5K. He never imagined being able to run to the end of the street before he started but now it was over three miles. Little and often.

His Mum's part-time home-based business was working by fitting in little bits of activity around her busy life. Making a quick call, sending a text and having a conversation over a coffee.

And then Milo was aware that by reading this book, over the past three weeks, he was making small changes in his life such as drinking less fizzy drinks, writing things down, thinking before speaking and being aware of what people are saying.

Everything was starting to make sense in his mind now. There wasn't going to be a quick fix, his everyday choices would affect a long-term result and, as long as the choices were positive, it is OK not to know what direction you are heading sometimes. Some students in school get really stressed if they don't know exactly what they want to do in the future. He also noticed that teachers and adults seem to quit things because they don't think they are making progress and they can't see instant results of success.

Milo realised that the small choices, decisions and commitments he had made over the past month since picking up the Future Toolbox were already beginning to show slight changes in him as a person.

Ah yes, he remembered seeing a relative at a family party last month. His Aunty Mabel ran over to him squealing with excitement. "Ooh, haven't you grown? The last time I saw you, you were only this high," she held her hand about 50 cm from the floor. Truth is, Milo hadn't grown over one metre overnight of course. His mum, dad, sister and everyone who saw him daily wouldn't have noticed the dramatic change but his aunt who hadn't seen him for years had noticed his slight, unnoticeable daily growth compounded over time.

Penny or millions.

There is a marvellous and way of bringing to life how the **compound effect** works using money and it is a story we have heard from many others and shared ourselves in our sessions with thousands of people.

The question is, if you were to be offered £1 **million** in cash now or a **penny** that doubled every day for a month, what would you take?

Milo remembered this exercise in the first Future Toolbox **session at school last month. He recalled the conversation with Rico and their mates around them.**

"Million for me," said Rico, "I'm going to be an instant millionaire!"

"Yeah, me too!" said Milo, "I'll have some of that."

Fidelma took the penny that day.

It turned out that if you take a penny and double it every day for a month, in thirty-one days' time it will be worth £10,737,418. Most people would take the million and look for instant success.

What, over £10m? Yes, that's right. This is a great analogy of the little things making big differences over a long period of time. A penny will become two on day two. On day three, four pence, and day four, eight pence. This is not a great deal of money but the magic is in the amount of increase, it is doubling. By day ten it will be worth £5.12. Most people will quit a habit in the first stage of their journey, **the really painful and unbearable stage.** The amount of result seen is so small that they question if the effort is worth it.

By day twenty, the amount will now be £5,242. In **H is for Habits**, this represents **the uncomfortable stage** and people still quit here. They may cash in the money or in real life, they have seen a few changes but the prize and reward for their effort isn't big enough so they decide to quit.

It isn't until day twenty-eight when the money actually overtakes the £1 million-pound mark and becomes £1,342,177.28. At this point, 97% of people will have quit but the remaining 3% will stick with their goals, keep working on their positive habits and see their goal out. The final total in this little exercise is £10,737,418.24.

OK, it is going to be very difficult to make this amount of money in such a short space of time but the most exciting moral behind this story is the fact that it is only the same amount of maths daily, the money was doubled. Imagine if it was smaller and we started with one tenth of a penny, you would still end up with over £1 million pounds. Or in real life, if you were able to improve by 0.01% in many areas of your life on a daily basis? How much would you improve in a year? Don't worry about the maths, just keep it simple and be consistent and you will see magnificent results.

Story of two friends, Hugo and Gary.
Let's finish with a story of two friends. **Hugo** reads and listens to motivational things every day, cuts 125 calories from his diet (which is about the same as a quarter of a bar of chocolate), drinks at least two litres of water and walks an extra 2,000 steps (one mile) to his daily routine.

Gary watches reality TV shows and reads the daily newspapers. He misses a few workouts a week, eats junk food in the office whilst drinking fizzy drinks and spends most of his time sitting in his chair.

In six months time, both of the friends appear exactly the same as they did on day one. Even a year later it may be difficult to see any huge change. However, fast forward two years. **Hugo** has now read over forty-five books and listened to over 450 hours of motivational content. **Gary** is watching the next TV show and is still moaning about the world.

Hugo has saved consuming over 90,000 calories which is equal to around 12 kg (26 lbs) of fat. **Gary** has gained at least this and more, in fact he is now 12 kg (2 st) overweight.

In just the extra 1,000 steps taken, **Hugo** has now walked over an extra 700 miles and **Gary** is still paying the gym membership but never goes plus he is out of breath when walking up the stairs.

Hugo has been promoted in his job, is paid more, is enjoying new challenges and has loads of energy every day. **Gary** is still in a rut, doesn't like his job and dreads going to work but has no idea how to change it so spends most of his time complaining about it to everyone.

These are true of millions of people on this planet and it all starts with a choice. Which path would you like to follow? The small **positive** choices over time will lead you to where you want to be.

Milo's Toolbox:

The little things are important. I must be disciplined not to skip the small tasks daily because I think it doesn't matter. Think about the little decisions and choices I make every day and be aware if they are positive or negative.

I will continue to eat well, drink plenty of water, exercise and be on time.

Keep hitting the pause button to listen before speaking.

Milo Challenges You:

Think about the decisions you are making on a daily basis and the small improvements that you could make.

What one thing could you change about what you eat?

What do you read, listen to or watch? Could you change something negative to a positive? The hourly news on the radio and the newspaper for instance, are full of shocking and depressing headlines. Could you listen to or read something inspirational instead?

Could you walk instead of going by motorised transport?

Could you be five minutes early instead of five minutes late?

Could you avoid spending a couple of pounds a day on, say that coffee from the shop? Perhaps you could make your own coffee?

Could you pop a pen in your pocket or bag instead of saying that you haven't got a pen?

Pick one small choice and take out your mobile phone. Set a daily reminder to carry out this task and then follow it. Try the thirty-day habit challenge we talked about in **H is for Habits**.

Refer back to your journal entries that you have been keeping and check that you are still on track. What difference are you making to your life?

Fun Facts – Things that become worth loads (or not)

According to Investopedia, if your grandparents had invested $40 (around £30) into a single share of Coca-Cola in 1919, your investment would be worth $394,352 (around £300,000) today. Coca-Cola calculated, if you had reinvested all dividends paid on the share over the years then it would now be worth $9.8 million (around £7.4m). Shame nobody could predict the future.

We talked about the cost of a mobile phone in the Needs versus Wants section and just to cover ourselves, there are examples of how to make money out of that old handset. Some of the really old ones, yep ones not cool anymore, are collectible. A 1983 Motorola DynaTAC 8000X, one of the first wireless phones ever made, recently sold at auction for £415.

Talking about taking the penny and doubling it for thirty-one days, well this didn't quite make as much but a one cent coin dated 1793 once sold on eBay for $49,500 (£37,500). That's not a bad return over a few hundred years. The first ever volume of *Playboy* Magazine with Marilyn Monroe on the cover fetched $6,795 on the site. An original Game Boy console with the game Tetris was bought for over £700 but it certainly didn't cost that new in 1989.

According to a report in the *Telegraph*, in 2004, David Brackin and Fraser Pearce set up a business selling other people's junk on eBay. They started in a spare bedroom and have since sold over £7m of stock making a profit of around £2.5m. In that time, they have surely benefitted from the **compound effect** on bidding.

Looking for a profit? Well here is a list of items that have been known to consistently increase in value over the years: rare baseball cards, rare comic books, land, property, rare stamps, rare coins, gold & silver. Please, please don't go out and buy loads of these items though, only rare and mint condition versions usually fetch big money and it is not guaranteed that these trends will continue. Property, land and suchlike can drop in value too as can stocks and shares, investments always carry a risk.

On the other hand, according to a report in the *Guardian*, some things that usually decrease in value are: cars – the Chevrolet Spark was reported to cost just under £10,000 new and would fetch £2,800 only three years later, wedding dresses new can cost over £1,000+ and a day later be sold for £100, computer games such as FIFA 16 cost £56 new and was on sale for £10 when FIFA 17 was launched, similarly, mobile smartphones can cost hundreds of pounds new but drop dramatically when the next version is launched.

B is for Belief – Fixed or Growth Mindsets

"We are what we think. All that we are arises with our thoughts. With our thoughts we make our world." – The Buddha (Founder of Buddhism)

A meeting had been arranged during morning break on Thursday for the students on the Future Toolbox **Programme. Their coaches were visiting school the next day for a follow-up session with them and the teachers. Ice Man Isaac read out the email from the coaches with some simple instructions:**

Hello amazing Future Toolbox **students.**

We are really excited to see you all tomorrow for a fabulous Friday.

Today we would like you to read your journal and reflect on what you have written. Think about the things you have learnt about yourself. What tools have you added to your toolbox?

You may also nominate an extra student to come along to the session, someone who you think would benefit from hearing about what you have learnt too. Let Mrs Lombardi or Mr Switchblade know who and they will sort this out.

Have a great evening and see you in the morning.

It all sounded simple enough and each and everyone agreed to talk in twos or threes later to compare notes. Milo nominated Rico to come to the session after he had started asking some questions. Mrs Lombardi agreed and Rico was invited. They were both delighted that he accepted.

That evening after reading through his journal, Milo called Fidelma to see what she had learnt.

"This is much better than revision, isn't it?" she said.

"Anything is better than revision but this stuff is really useful. It's made me get less annoyed with my sister for sure," he chuckled. "She isn't as irritating as she once was. Perhaps the magic is working on her."

"I'm not eating so much rubbish now," Fidelma continued. "That bloke was right about you having more energy, wasn't he? And the sleep stuff too. It's hard not to watch TV or chat before bed but I'm not as much of a moody cow in the mornings anymore," she laughed.

Milo made the decision to become an entrepreneur.

"Who invented that word though, I can never spell it?"

"The French probably."

"Yeah, true. Anyway, I helped Mum with another business presentation yesterday and really enjoyed it. I never thought I would enjoy hanging out with my mum so much," he said lowering his voice just in case she could hear.

Fidelma was really working on her confidence and self-belief, trying to say I can more instead of I can't.

The Friday feeling.

"Hey guys, welcome to Friday. One of the greatest days of the week. Who doesn't like Mondays though? That day after the weekend when we all return to school or work after having some quality time for ourselves."

Some hands were raised. "If your hand is up, we need to change your mindset and make Mondays great." A few sceptical faces in the group of thirty students struggled to cope with the idea of being so positive after a long weekend. "Yep, you're all probably feeling a little negative now we have talked about Monday but let's have a look at ways we can change how we feel about something by simply changing the way we feel."

The next instruction was to break into pairs, including the teachers, and then chat about some situations with personal experiences. Milo paired up with Fidelma, it made sense as they had chatted the night before and worked through the programme together from the start.

Rico ended up sitting with Ice Man Isaac, who didn't suffer fools. There would be little chance of him piping up with his wise jokes and silly comments. Looking across at Milo and Fidelma, he shot a disapproving look knowing that he now had to take the session a little more seriously.

A **fixed mindset** is a little like the dead branches on a tree. If the tree is not watered and nourished properly then it will eventually dry up and rot away.

A **growth mindset** is like an evergreen tree that grows and grows. The branches grow thicker and the leaves fuller as new buds continue to sprout. A tree never gets to a certain height and decides to have a week off growing or stop altogether. That is Mother Nature at her best!

Here are things we face every day in life; **challenges and obstacles, effort, critics and other people**. They will influence our results and success depending on our mindset. This is a good time to think about your own examples in your own life.

Challenges and obstacles.
A **fixed mindset** will avoid them, perhaps for the fear of failure and because they aren't lucky enough. This will cause this person to give up easily and quit. Have you ever quit something because you feel you are failing?

A **growth mindset** will thrive on a challenge and **persist in the face of setbacks**. Things will be tough but focussing on the end goal will get you there. What are you succeeding in now?

Milo knew his biggest obstacle was procrastination and distraction. He chatted to Fidelma about his English project the other week, it was a disaster but he dug in and pulled it around. He could have quit of course but he didn't and completed it. Also, there was his friend's mum who said she couldn't run her own business, what she meant was she wouldn't and closed the door by creating an obstacle.

Fidelma pointed out that the famous people in F is for Failure all overcame obstacles. JK Rowling being rejected by twelve publishers, Col. Sanders being told 1,009 times that his fried chicken recipe wasn't good enough and Disney being fired for not being creative enough, apparently.

Effort.

A **fixed** mindset will see effort as too hard and it doesn't matter how hard I try, it will never work. What is the point is doing this, if I miss something then it won't make any difference? Have you ever given up too easily?

A **growth mindset** will see every piece of effort will **lead to mastery** and the big results will follow. Have you achieved a big goal after a long period of hard effort?

"Easy," said Fidelma, "We had C is for Compound Effect! Doing those things that we can't be bothered to do on a daily basis will affect our success. I have to stop saying that I can't be bothered so much and actually be bothered."

"And there is P is for Practice," Milo added, glancing over at Switchblade knowing he was probably talking about press-ups. Yep, he was!

The masters put in the effort, practice and over time, this leads to their success. **Why do nothing when you can do something?** We have asked this before but have you noticed that when you do nothing, nothing happens? How many times have you said, "I can't be bothered?" A little effort goes a long way, what could you put a little more effort into? Remember, remove I can't, I won't and I don't know from your daily language where possible.

How do successful people become a success? That's right, a whole bucket load of effort compounded over time. Singers practise, actors rehearse, sports stars train, business people work hard...

Ever been to a great party? Did the party happen or did it need a lot of planning? Find venue, when to hold it, sort music, what food, who to invite, what to wear...

Had a holiday before? It needed effort to save, book, plan, buy essentials, pack and get there before you could start enjoying it.

Milo told Fidelma about his training sessions with the cross-country team, sometimes in the cold and wet. Times when he couldn't be bothered or wanted to stay home or even quit. He finished his 5K and beat his dad of course.

Criticism.
A **fixed mindset** will argue with or hit back at the critics and see it as a negative. Normally this will lead to the person getting defensive or perhaps blaming something else. When was the last time you hit back at a critic and blamed something or someone else?

The **growth mindset** will allow you to **learn from mistakes**. The criticism was a piece of feedback to build on and move forward. When have you learnt from and seen critical feedback and a positive step towards success?

We know that we can't blame the traffic or the bus for making us late? OK, sometimes things are completely unavoidable but the majority of the time it is actually your fault. Easy to leave earlier or easy not to, it's up to you.

Remember:
- **T is for Time**, did you plan properly?
- **R is for Response-Ability**, how did you respond to a task?
- **Q is for Quality**, did you do your best?
- **N is for No Time Like the Present**, did you procrastinate?

Fidelma and Milo both swung around and looked at Rico. He was listening to Ice Man Isaac, who seemed to be doing most of the talking.

"He's always blaming others, isn't he? The bus made him late, his mum moved his homework pile, the teacher didn't tell him the instructions that everyone else heard. He even blames me sometimes," said Milo, pointing his finger forward at Rico as he looked up to catch Milo's accusation. He gestured a look of, what me, how dare you before grinning knowing that he had been caught, guilty as charged.

Fidelma certainly didn't like to be criticised either, "I always get defensive, especially when I am told that something isn't to the best of my ability. This is Mrs Lombardi's most used phrase isn't it and it always irritates me so I always try and find an excuse when she says it."

Milo then held his hands out wide, "Of course, my planning has improved since I started doing my weekly planner. I mean it's not perfect but it's a start. At least I don't forget everything I need to do now."

Success of others.
The **fixed mindset** will feel threatened by successful people and could lack confidence. When did you last say, "I can never be that good?"

A **growth mindset** will see successful people as **inspirational role models to learn from**. Who was the last successful person you studied? Someone who was good at something and had good habits.

Milo told Fidelma that he had looked at the way she planned her studies and copied those habits which have helped.

"We're also copying the habits in the Future Toolbox, **aren't we? These are all used by successful people, some famous and some that we don't hear their names."**

Rico was now mimicking an air guitar action to Ice Man Isaac, it was clear that he was talking about copying one of his favourite guitar heroes to practise. Ice Man Isaac gave him an approving expression.

"Excellent, Rico is learning from Ice Man Isaac now, look at him having a serious conversation over there."

In life, people become victims of circumstances. This means that fixed mindsets start to own them and become their boss. I bet you have friends who are SAD? No, not sad as in the slang meaning that they are interested in things that are classed as boring. SAD as in people who are affected by things like bad weather, grey skies and Mondays.

According to mental health charity Mind, seasonal affective disorder (SAD) is a form of depression that people experience at a particular time of year or during a particular season. It is a recognised mental health disorder. Most of us are affected by the change in seasons – it is normal to feel more cheerful and energetic when the sun is shining and the days are longer, or to find that you eat more or sleep longer in winter. However, if you experience SAD, the change in seasons will have a much greater effect on your mood and energy levels, and lead to symptoms of depression that may have a significant impact on your day-to-day life. Perhaps by changing our mindset on a day of the week like Monday or a dull, rainy day can help. Those days are out of our control and will happen whether we choose to be happy or sad.

We talked about anxiety and stress in **M is for Meditation** and also established that we can't control the laws of our wonderful planet and change the weather. These are uncontrollables that affect us all the same. Creating a **growth mindset** will help to create a positive outlook, move forward in life and relieve stress along the way.

As the session drew to a close, Milo went over to the Future Toolbox **coaches and shook their hands.**

"Thank you for another great session and helping me out so much. I'm enjoying this journey."

"That's fantastic, that means a lot to us." was the reply. "We have had to create growth mindsets many times in order to be successful ourselves. We still sometimes think that we can't do something or that it isn't good enough. That is life. Keep setting your goals and working towards them."

Just then Rico appeared and instead of putting his arm around Milo's neck or shoving him in the arm, he offered a handshake and a thank you. Milo looked a little shocked at first because there was normally some poor joke or smart comment coming from his

mouth but instead he said; "So, I now know that if I keep practising my guitar then I can learn any tune I want. I can join a band and write my own music. I've never had the confidence to do that before."

Rico was always keen to spend his life living in a tour bus and rolling in millions of pounds of bank notes but he was now talking like a different person. "Music is fantastic, I really enjoy playing it but understand that I may not enjoy travelling all over the world all the time. I think I would like to maybe learn how to be a brilliant guitarist and help others to learn how to play it too. Perhaps that could be a good plan if I don't become famous."

Mrs Lombardi stopped in her tracks as she heard these words coming from Rico and she was in a small state of shock. He may be great fun but Rico was usually thinking of himself but now to admit to consider helping others was a side that none of them had seen or heard before.

The Future Toolbox coaches smiled, sort of knowing that they sometimes see the full potential of someone in a moment. "Good for you man, stay focussed on the goals but keep enjoying what you enjoy!"

Milo's Toolbox:
It's all in the mindset.
Look at ways of growing every day.
I will use others as inspiration and realise that my critics are usually helping me to improve.

If I am my own biggest critic then I will remove some of the pressure by looking at a way to move forward and make positive improvements.

Milo Challenges You:
Look at the table below and make a note of at least one instance of when you have followed the path of a fixed mindset. Read the chapter above and answer the questions below each description and example if that helps.

	Fixed	**Growth**
Challenges and obstacles	Avoid them and give up easily	Embrace them and persist
Effort	Too hard, give up easily	Every piece of effort leads to mastery
Criticism	Resent or blame	Learn from mistakes
Success of others	I can never be that good	Inspired by others

Now look at a way of moving the fixed into growth mindsets by overcoming the obstacles and challenges, putting in a little more effort, seeing your critics as feedback and being inspired by others.

Fun Facts — Strangest beliefs
In this chapter we have talked about belief in yourself. Your subconscious mind can't tell the difference between something that is real or made up, that means positive thinking is technically tricking your brain into being successful.
However, people generally believe what they hear and the world loves a good conspiracy theory. Here are some of the most well-known.

- Elvis died in 1977 and rapper Tupac in 1996 but many people believe that they are still alive. There are still millions of sightings of Elvis – The King reported every year. Staying on the topic of world-famous people, one of the most famous conspiracy theories surrounded Princess Diana, who was tragically killed in 1997. Some believe that Diana wanted to escape the public eye and the crash was to fake her death. Other rumours claim that the accident was a set up by British Intelligence acting on behalf of the Royal Family because they didn't want the Al-Fayed family connecting with them. May Elvis, Tupac and Diana R.I.P. and their legacies live on.

- We all learn about him in school but there are beliefs that the world's greatest author wasn't who he claimed to be. William Shakespeare of Stratford wasn't the writer of these celebrated plays, conspiracy theorists say the works were actually written by William Stanley or Francis Bacon.

- Ever looked into the sky and seen those little white lines left behind the flight paths of aeroplanes? This is caused by the vapour from the plane's exhaust hitting the cold air and condensing to leave a trail. That's the short scientific explanation, however, some paranoid folk are convinced that the government is spraying chemical agents at its citizens from 30,000 feet.

- Flick a switch and on comes the light! Thomas Edison's invention all those years ago has now evolved into LEDs but it's still believed that the lightbulb industry manufactures bulbs with a shorter shelf life than possible so they blow and you have to buy more. This similar theory applies to technology updates from Android, Apple, Windows and suchlike. Claims that updating your software will inject bugs into your devices making them run slower so you buy new ones. Nothing seems to last these days does it?

- "One small step for man!" These words were uttered by Neil Armstrong in 1969 as he stepped onto the moon but it is one of the most popular conspiracy theories of all time. Many believe that the moon landing was a hoax and he made one small step onto a film set here on planet Earth.

- We are not alone though! Going into space, is there alien life form out there? Back in 1947, an unknown object crashed into the ground near Roswell, New Mexico. Since then, hundreds of conspiracy theories have been created, many telling us it was a UFO. A secret base known as Area 51 is close by and the US government claimed there was no such place until 2003 when they finally admitted it was real. This has all fuelled the world's obsession with aliens and UFOs.

- Talking of the American government, another theory surrounded the actual events that caused the World Trade Centre to collapse in the 9/11 atrocities. The most popular beliefs are that the towers were blown up by an explosive on the ground or the planes seen flying into the towers were actually missiles.

Your mind will choose what you tell it to believe.

A is for Aha Moments – Yeah, I Get It

"The greatest discovery of all time is that a person can change their future by merely changing their attitude." – Oprah Winfrey (talk show host, actress, producer)

"Knowing yourself is the beginning of all wisdom." – Aristotle (ancient Greek philosopher and scientist)

The penny drops, a light bulb moment or maybe you have seen the light? It is that moment when you go, "Aha, I get it!"

Mr Switchblade wandered to the front of the room. "If I could all have a moment with you before you leave," everyone grabbed a seat. Switch smiled a huge smile and looked around the room at each and every student and teacher whilst nodding his head in approval. There was a sense of anticipation as the group waited for his first words. Finally, he broke what seemed like an eternity of silence.

"Wow, what can I say? Thank you to our Future Toolbox coaches for giving us all the opportunity to use their tools. Some of you here have made some small changes and some of you big. You all volunteered to take part in this programme and you now all have a choice of what you do with this in your lives ahead of you. We promised you a reward at the end of this chapter in your journey and here it is."

He gestured to the coaches to join him again at the front and he moved aside to let them speak.

"OK, let's finish on this note. You have a reward that isn't a financial or a material prize, we have given you a book and a journal which you have read and written in. You now have something valuable and that is wisdom and success tips to use in your future."

A couple of students looked a little disappointed at first as there was no physical reward. "The reward is that your journey will continue and you get to write what happens next in your life story. As Mr Switchblade said, this is only the first chapter that is complete. You are now equipped with life skills and tools to put into your toolbox. Use them, enjoy them and be the best person you can be."

Those disappointed faces broke into smiles and a round of applause broke out. Milo turned to Fidelma and said loudly, "Aha, I get it!"

Later that evening he turned to the final chapter in the Future Toolbox **book and read.**

The magic happens.
It is a magical time when, suddenly, the bigger picture evolves in your mind and makes you go, "Ahaaaaaaaa!"

A great example of this is a famous story of a Greek called Archimedes, who discovered how to measure the volume of an irregular object whilst taking a bath. He noticed that water flooded over the edge when his body sank into the tub, all he would have to do is measure the volume of water displaced and that would equal the volume of the body immersed in the water. At that point he jumped out of the bath and ran home naked shouting "Eureka" (I found it).

Now Archimedes may have got away with the famous "eureka" moment of running through the streets naked but most of us would probably be arrested these days.

Sometimes we have to seize the **aha moment** and take this idea or this ray of light forward. Write down the idea and store it for later if the time isn't right.

The best ideas pop into your head from time to time when you are least expecting it. You may think of the best idea whilst sitting on the bus or in traffic, midway through a lesson or even in the middle of the night. If this is the case, simply scribble down a keyword and act on it later.

Perhaps you have found an **aha moment** or two in this book.

Milo's Toolbox:

Now I have completed this chapter in my life journey, it is time to write the next one·

Look at my goals, focus on positive thinking and create a growth mindset in order to achieve the end result·

Enjoy the journey along the way and keep doing the little things that will get me there·

Keep on studying success and developing my life skills·

I have the ability to be a success and be in control of my own destiny·

Milo Challenges You:

As you end this journey, Milo challenges you to write your next chapter.

Make a note of the **aha moments** you have taken from this book. They may be things that you never knew before but most likely, they could be skills you knew of, already possess but have perhaps fallen off the wagon and need to climb back on.

Take small steps to improve yourself daily. Continue to practise in **personal development**, maybe read another book, listen to an audio version or watch one in video format.

Now finish off by writing down one seriously big, amazingly outrageous and extremely exciting goal.

Fun Facts – Eureka, accidental discoveries

Archimedes had his eureka moment at an unexpected time and it is no surprise to learn that most everyday objects we take for granted these days were also discovered by accident.

Alexander Fleming saved millions of lives thanks to a botched experiment. After going on holiday without doing the washing up, he returned to discover a mould growing on his petri dishes in his laboratory. Bizarrely no bacteria had grown. **Aha**, the first antibiotic, penicillin!

Fancy a packet of salt & vinegar or cheese & onion? Thank George Crum for that one. He was that irritating customer who kept sending his potatoes back to the kitchen claiming they were too thick. The irritated chef sliced the potatoes thinner than wafers and roasted them as a joke. Mr Crum actually loved them so much, they became a speciality and the popularity grew from there.

A guy called Robert Chesebrough went on a mission to get rich from an oil discovery back in 1859. In the oil fields he noticed that workers were complaining about an annoying, waxy substance, known as rod wax, that gummed up their drilling equipment. Chesebrough decided to call it Vaseline and he used it to treat cuts and burns. He even ate a spoonful of it every day. Bizarre but true.

And there's more. Velcro was discovered by Swiss engineer George de Mestral when he found burrs from the grass clinging to his dog's fur. On closer inspection, he found that the burrs' hooks would cling to anything loop-shaped. If he could only artificially re-create the loops, he might be on to something.

Coca-Cola wasn't ever planned as a soft drink, pharmacist John Pemberton just wanted to find a way to cure headaches. He mixed accidentally coca leaves and cola nuts with carbonated water and the world's first Coke was the result.

Post-it notes were another "**aha moment**" in 1968 when Spencer Silver discovered "low tack" sticky stuff but thought it useless. His buddy Art

Fry was always irritated with not having sticky notes for his church books. They added both two and here we are.

When Will Keith Kellogg was actually looking for a good cereal recipe in 1895 he forgot about some boiled wheat he left sitting out. The wheat became disgustingly flaky looking but the result was a whole heap of Corn Flakes.

Sometimes that light bulb moment will happen when you least expect it. Saccharin, an artificial sweetener was discovered by Constantin Fahlberg who didn't wash his hands before eating. A chemical product he had been using made his wife's freshly made biscuits taste sweeter than usual, thankfully it didn't kill him.

Even Play-Doh was created to be a cleaning product to clean dirty wallpapers and kids have enjoyed creating stuff out of it for years, not to mention eating it. Sometimes you just never know what you will discover but most of all, make sure you keep working on yourself and discover your true self.

Sometime in the Future

Hey everyone, it's Milo again. School is now becoming a distant memory for me as I am sitting at home with my Future Toolbox book and journal on the table in front of me. Six months has since passed and I am reflecting on my journey so far. The once very shy and quiet student now has a new confidence as I continue to grow. Yes, grow up physically of course but the best thing is developing as a person. My story now is about my change in belief, yes that is **B is for Belief**... changing from fixed to growth mindsets.

After picking up his certificates on results day at school, Milo was reasonably pleased to have passed his qualifications. Since discovering the **Future Toolbox**, he could look himself in the eye in the mirror and say, "I gave it my best shot!" *(**I is for "I Am the Greatest"** and **Q is for Quality**)*

So where is Milo now? Well he is still working in Lois Latte's coffee shop and loving learning new skills. Lois has left him in charge at times, he continues to develop his customer-service skills and is learning how a small business works. (**J is for Job Satisfaction**)

One day Thea's friend Melissa came into the coffee shop and her and Milo came up with an idea on how to make some really healthy, organic snacks that could be sold in the shop. He spoke to Lois about the idea and she asked for some samples. Melissa, Thea and Milo made some and they became an instant hit with the customers. Lois then agreed that she would pay Milo 10% of the profits of any of the snacks sold. Melissa and Thea now work in the shop at the weekend preparing the ingredients for the week's production. The idea was so successful that Lois is now looking to supply the snacks to other local places like Father Russmuss's Food Box and Big Dan's Bowling Alley. (**O is for Open Your Mind** and **V is for Vegetables**)

This is Milo's first step towards his goal of becoming an entrepreneur and he is sharing the profits with Melissa and Thea of course. (**G is for Goals**).

With the money he is making from the profits as well as the tips he gets from customers, Milo now saves 25% of everything he earns. That means for every £100 he is paid, he puts £25 into a savings account. After visiting his local bank and having an appointment with Carol Cashier, he has found the best way of saving his money so he can get the best possible rate of interest paid. It is only a small amount but he understands the value of the compound effect. (**W is for Wonga** and **C is for Compound Effect**)

When spending money, Milo always asks the question, "Do I really need this?" Sometimes the answer is yes and sometimes it is no. If it's no, he then makes the choice whether he should spend the money as a treat or not. It's a great habit to have. (**D is for Desires** and **H is for Habits**)

When he isn't working, Milo loves his fitness plan. He trains with the local athletics club with Ice Man Isaac. They have become really good friends and they help motivate each other to train, even in the bad weather and cold nights. Now that there are no PE teachers at school, it is their own responsibility to train and not to miss sessions because they can't be bothered. Yep, the ability to respond. (**E is for Exercise** and **R is for Response-Ability**)

Milo is benefitting from the regular practice in training sessions, his race times are getting quicker and he is feeling fitter. Isaac helps him with his confidence but he also listens to the top runners and coaches at the club who work to develop the younger runners' abilities. (**P is for Practice** and **L is for Listening**)

His dad is also a member of the running club so family competition is still strong. Milo knows he can always beat his dad but he loves to encourage him too. They have both been offered the opportunity to enter some competitions through the club. About a year ago, Milo would have said no way but with his growth mindset, he now knows he can do it. The opportunity came along and he seized it, entering straight away. (**U is for U Can Do It** and **N is for No Time Like the Present**)

All this training may sound like hard work but Milo still enjoys resting and chilling out on the sofa to watch TV. He does eat much healthier after learning lots from Melissa and the healthy snacks they make at work and he knows how much he needs to have the energy to get through each day. However, he still finds time to relax and meditate quietly daily plus continuing his personal development to learn new things. (**V is for Vegetables** and **M is for Meditation**)

He has a busy life with all this working, training, learning and relaxing but he finds to time socialise with friends too. First the learning, he still uses his weekly planner to list down things that need to be done and to set short and long-term goals. His journal is full of quotes and notes of things he has learned from his mum's part-time business which is going from strength to strength. He has even looked at ways to become involved in the future. (**T is for Time** and **O is for Open Your Mind**)

He and his mum do sit down and listen to and watch inspirational audios and videos by successful people. Their affirmation is, "We will do our best to be our best selves!" (**I is for "I Am the Greatest"** and **Q is for Quality**)

Socially, he is still good friends with Rico but Rico has had to learn from quite a few mistakes. Firstly, he failed his qualifications and was given the choice to re-sit them. He decided not to. On another occasion, he decided to go into the coffee shop to see Milo whilst he was at work. Messing around, he managed to upset and offend two customers who were having a meeting over a coffee. They complained to Lois Latte about Milo having his mates there and said it wasn't professional. Although it wasn't exactly Milo's fault, he had to take some of the blame because he was laughing and joking with Rico and this was one of the things that upset the customers.

Lois wasn't pleased of course as it was against the rules to have friends in the shop hanging around unless they were paying customers. Rico wasn't that day, he was just hanging around for quite some time and just chatting. Milo had broken a rule and had to take responsibility. (**X is for X-Rated**)

He decided to respond by giving the customers some of his free health snacks and coffee on their next visit, paid for out of his own pocket of course. The customer accepted Milo's apology and all is forgiven. However, it turns out that the customer was a guy called Vic The Vocalist, local musician who was meeting with a music promoter Oscar Octave at the time. Rico blew his chance to impress two people who could have perhaps opened a door for him to make a step towards his dream of being a guitarist in a band. He now has to think before he opens his mouth and makes a stupid comment that might offend someone. (**R is for Response-Ability** and **F is for Failure**)

Milo still watches the TV now and again and *Lily the Looter's Virtual Crime World* is still a favourite in their household, He still has the dream of being a guitar hero but hasn't yet begun learning to play even though Rico keeps offering to teach him. He knows he can't physically be his guitar hero and he needs to change his mindset to, "I can play the guitar" but it remains on his goal list. (**Y is for Your Life** and **G is for Goals**)

His body clock is still working at times but the sleep hygiene still needs a little attention when there are weekend parties. Of course, we deserve a party and a late night now and again and why not have a lie in at times? (**Z is for ZZZ**)

One person who hasn't yet been mentioned is Fidelma. Well she decided to study a part-time adult-education programme whilst working beginning her career. After finishing school, her and Milo have remained good friends after sharing the **Future Toolbox** journey closely together. It was a real aha moment that they realised that they had so much in common in their views and goals. (**A is for Aha Moments** and **S is for Smile**)

In **K is for Kiss and Make Up**, we talked about appreciating people and, perhaps it was the laws of attraction that made them end up as good friends. Well everyone loves a happy ending so Milo and Fidelma, we're not going to spread any rumours here but we'll let you make up the ending.

Meet the Future Toolbox Coaches

How would I describe myself? My name is Mark and I am a motivational speaker, life teacher, network marketing professional, business owner who has fun working in a sociable environment. Since the mid-1990s I have worked with thousands of teenagers and adults as a careers coach, motivational speaker and educational trainer and facilitator.

Leaving school with a couple of GCSEs, my education can only be described as... erm... hold on... it was just very unfocussed. I was a quiet sixteen-year-old, barely in trouble and never one to speak out loud much.

My first career choices were bank manager, estate agent or teacher. The latter needed a degree, so I decided on the others but had no idea why, my family said they were good choices I guess. In business studies, I even designed a logo for MK Estate Agents but that venture never came off.

I was told you study hard, get a good job and work your way up the career ladder to become a manager. Go to work wearing a suit and get promoted. Promotions lead to pay rises. Invest into a good pension plan and retire at sixty-five. So my first job was working in a building society, sorting mortgage statements. Yep sounds boring, but everyone has to start somewhere.

One thing I possessed from an early age is the intrigue to find out how things worked and why was I sorting those bits of paper out. What was the purpose? This ethic of being willing to learn led to some promotions which took me on a journey through the building society, then estate agency and next insurance before securing a job for a recruitment and training company for teenagers. It was rewarding to help hundreds of people start their careers by helping them plan for their first interview, understand the basic life skills in the work place and then how to develop a good work ethic.

Here I met my wife Jules who was the training manager; her job was to manage the apprenticeship training side of the business. She helped hundreds of young people gain further-education qualifications in business and childcare and realise their ambitions. In 2009 we set up our own motivational training company called MAD4Life and developed the **Future Toolbox** to help teenagers and adults make choices and decisions to change their lives.

On this journey, we discovered personal development and the process of setting goals, focussing on positive thinking and continuing to learn and improve yourself on a daily basis. All of these aspects are keys to be a successful person.

Yep, I had a big shift in direction and skill set but it did not happen overnight. As a kid I had no goal to do this. In fact, there was no defined goal. Being far too quiet, always average at everything and never in trouble and with little confidence... to give a seminar to 400 people was too far off the radar, in fact, I wouldn't even speak in front of the class or take part in a school play.

The thought of growing up was scary and sounded sometimes boring. Doing things like paying bills, ironing (not that we do much of that) and owning a house seemed dull and the word "responsibility" was simply frightening.

It is the small changes and life lessons that make success happen and Jules and I are proud to call ourselves extremely successful people.

We are not materialistic people or even millionaires. We do not drive fast cars, own speedboats or live in a huge mansion. Those are not really our things.

We enjoy creating great experiences for us and our family to enjoy, living a stress-free lifestyle and collecting great memories.

Our passions are travelling the world — we have been on many trips to some amazing places, from a week on the beach to a city break to a backpacking adventure, it is our passion to enjoy experiencing real cultures. Health and fitness are important as is eating lovely healthy food and watching our incredible family develop.

We are excited for you already. Let us step into the world and learn from some of the best teachers ever. We haven't invented this stuff, we just study the success habits of successful people and follow them. If you find something good then share it with others (and that's what we are doing for you now).

Enjoy creating your life journey...

Website: **www.futuretoolbox.co.uk**

Social media:

@futuretoolbox – Instagram – Twitter – Facebook

Acknowledgements

Writing this book has been like an amazing journey, it has been fun, exciting (sometimes frustrating and occasionally tiring) but most of all, eye-opening. From scribbling notes on scraps of paper to filling the notes section on a mobile phone, it wouldn't have been possible without the help of so many people who made this dream become a reality.

There are always so many people to thank but we'd like to start with Michael Wright and Melissa James of Millennial Creative who without them, we wouldn't be writing this now. We met them around three-quarters of the way into the manuscript and needed some inspiration to get us to the finish line. Their total understanding of what we were trying to achieve was completely pivotal. So, thank you for your creative inspiration, from the artwork that brought our lovable character Milo to life to the feedback on the writing styles. Milo is now a part of our everyday life.

It was a gift to meet Andy Gibney and Caroline Snelling at 3P Publishing. Thank you for working your magic by turning a Word document into the book that you now hold in your hands and giving us such invaluable guidance along the way.

We can't thank our wonderful friend Hazel Napier enough for proofreading the early draft chapters and not only giving us honest feedback but teaching us some new grammar techniques along with some crazy nights along the way!

Milo also wouldn't have been possible without Roger Taylor of the Website Business. Another good friend who was helping us with our website and designed the very first logo with the character in it that later became known as Milo.

Closer to home, to our family who have been brilliant in their support and feedback along the way. Special thanks to Roxanne, Lou, Russell, Daniel, Oli, Neil, Lois, Warwick, Ethan, Molly, Noah and of course, Mum.

Also, to our friends Monica, Lawrence, Kara, James, Phillipa, to name but a few for reading some chapters and scribbles.

When you want to become a master at something, then it is best to talk to the masters. Big thanks go to our good friend and best-selling author Wes Linden for your help, guidance and feedback along the way. Also, Barry The Book of Knowledge is King, we are so grateful for the tips, advice and factsheets you send us to make sure we are on the right track.

Finally, thank you to everyone who we have learnt from, those people who have inspired us in business, education, life, travel, sport, public speaking and in life in general, from the world leaders in personal development to the friends we see in the street, everyone has a story to share.

Oh, and we can't forget the wonderful beaches of the world where our minds can escape and give us freedom to write.

Testimonials

"I am generally a reluctant reader but this book engaged me and I found it clear throughout and well-constructed. The messages were useful and relevant and the humour used throughout the book helped make it engaging. The format was good and meant I could dip in and out of reading. The messages have a broader appeal than just for teenagers. In fact, my Mum is reading it now!" - James Campbell (aged 14)

"This book is honestly so good and I can say, hand on heart, I can take and use stuff from it in my life journey. I am proud to say that Don't Get Your Neck Tattooed has made such an impact on me." - Kara Milne (aged 12)

"As a university student, personal development and life skills are really important to make sure you stay on top of your work load.

Don't Get Your Neck Tattooed is a great way to be able to do this as it's not only full of really helpful hints and tricks but it's also really accessible too. It's great because you can pick it up at any chapter and run with the tools that are provided there, so if there are specific things you need to work on like your sleep hygiene or motivation, you can go straight to those chapters and find the help you need quickly. It's so full of great advice that you can go back to it time and again and find things you may have previously missed, the help from this book is never ending!

Don't Get Your Neck Tattooed is so digestible that it doesn't take too long to get through either which means you can use the productivity tips provided and get into action pretty quickly. In a nutshell it's a fantastic read and I highly recommend it to anybody looking to work on their personal development and life skills!" - Melissa James (Psychology & Counselling Student - University of Northampton)

"This is a brilliant guide for young people to thrive and get ahead in the 21st century.

Don't Get Your Neck Tattooed is a fabulous read for young people and adults alike. Mark and Jules's fun and humorous book is full of anecdotes and experiences that draw you in and keep you absorbed right to the end. Packed with thought provoking facts and ideas, it's a thoroughly good read and perfectly aimed at getting a young person's attention. I love Milo, the **Future Toolbox** character. Most of all, this book is uplifting and relatable. A must for every school library. Naomi Schaffer - (Careers Adviser)

"A great book for any teenager or young adult, packed full of life lessons." Barry Phillips – (Book Retailer)